Bob Dam

The Greatest Teachings of Jesus

The Greatest Teachings of Jesus

John Killinger

199 ₹

Abingdon Press
Nashville

BS2415 .K47 1993
Killinger, John.
The greatcal teachings of
Jesus

NGS OF JESUS

Copyright © ..... , bingdon Press

All rights reserved.
No part of this work may be reproduced or transmitted in any form or by any means, electronic or mechanical, including photocopying and recording, or by any information storage or retrieval system, except as may be expressly permitted by the 1976 Copyright Act or in writing from the publisher. Requests for permission should be addressed to Abingdon Press, 201 Eighth Avenue South, P.O. Box 801, Nashville TN 37202.

93 94 95 96 97 98 99 00 01 02—10 9 8 7 6 5 4 3 2 1

This book is printed on acid-free, recycled paper.

Library of Congress Cataloging-in-Publication Data

Killinger, John.
    The greatest teachings of Jesus/John Killinger.
    p.   cm.
    ISBN 0-687-15823-0 (alk. paper)
    1. Jesus Christ—Teachings.   I. Title.
    BS2415.K47   1993   93-12214
    230—dc20

Most scripture quotations are from the New Revised Standard Version Bible. Copyright 1989 by the Division of Christian Education of the National Council of the Churches of Christ in the USA. Used by permission.

Those noted RSV are from the Revised Standard Version of the Bible, Copyright 1946, 1952, 1971 by the Division of Christian Education of the National Council of Churches of Christ in the USA. Used by permission.

Those noted Phillips are from *The New Testament in Modern English*, Rev. Ed., by J. B. Phillips, Copyright © J. B. Phillips, 1958, 1959, 1960, 1972. Published by Macmillan Publishing Co., Inc., 1972.

MANUFACTURED IN THE UNITED STATES OF AMERICA

To my dear friends at the
First Congregational Church of Los Angeles,
and especially to my highly competent and
thoroughly delightful executive assistant,
Virginia Somerville,
who produced the manuscript for this book
and helped me to keep my life together in
the City of Angels

Contents

Introduction

The World's Greatest Teacher

Surely there can be no doubt in anyone's mind that Jesus of Nazareth was the greatest teacher the world has ever known. Today, nearly twenty centuries after he walked on the earth, his teachings continue to evoke more discussion than the combined teachings of Socrates, Buddha, Mohammed, and Marx. There are more books written about him each year than about any other person who ever lived. More courses in universities and institutions of higher learning are devoted to his ideas than to those of any other figure. The "shadow of illumination" which he has cast across the centuries and cultures of the world is quite simply beyond measure.

Why is this?

Jesus never wrote a book. He grew up in obscurity and lived and taught as an itinerant preacher outside the circle of tradition and acceptance. He died an outcast, condemned by the religious leaders of his nation.

For most teachers, such obstacles would have spelled certain failure. But for Jesus, they didn't.

Again we ask, Why?

There are some simple but very profound reasons for Jesus' influence.

HIS PRACTICAL AND PERSONAL MESSAGES

For one thing, the teachings of Jesus are invariably related to life. There is nothing precious or esoteric about them. Contrary to what one might expect, there is not even anything otherworldly about them. Whenever Jesus spoke, he spoke unwaveringly about the way we live and about how the way we live affects our happiness and well-being.

People respond to this kind of message. The worker in the mines, the secretary in the insurance company, the doctor in the operating room—all can relate to the sayings of Jesus. They find something vitally personal in them, as if Jesus were speaking directly to them about the things that matter most in their lives.

HIS BEAUTIFUL PROSE

Besides the practicality of the things Jesus said, there is the way he said them. His manner was never stilted or academic. He eschewed the more formal method preferred by the Greco-Roman culture of his day for the simple, memorable style of a traveling rabbi. His sayings are like jewels, sparkling with wit and truth:

"Blessed are the pure in heart, for they will see God" (Matt. 5:8).

"Do not store up for yourselves treasures on earth, where moth and rust consume and where thieves break in and steal; but store up for yourselves treasures in heaven, where neither moth nor rust consumes and where thieves do not break in and steal. For where your treasure is, there your heart will be also" (Matt. 6:19-21).

"Ask, and it will be given you; search, and you will find; knock, and the door will be opened for you. For everyone who asks receives, and everyone who searches finds, and for everyone who knocks, the door will be opened" (Matt. 7:7-8).

"If any want to become my followers, let them deny themselves and take up their cross and follow me. For those who want to save their life will lose it, and those who lose their life for my sake will find it" (Matt. 16:24-25)

His Unforgettable Stories

And Jesus' stories! They are like small dramas of the heart, each one arresting, penetrating, unforgettable. Their personae have become an indispensable part of the world's way of understanding itself—the good Samaritan, the prodigal son, the man who built his house on sand, the rich fool, the shepherd seeking his sheep, the wise and foolish virgins.

His Wonderful Example

It is also important that Jesus *lived* his teachings as well as taught them. It would be impossible to drive the thinnest blade between what he taught and how he acted. He was what he said, and he said what he was. When he died on the cross for love and obedience, it seemed the most natural thing in the world, for it was the inevitable consequence of everything he had taught about life and faith. He became the divine teacher to millions of people because his existence as a man was so transparent to the will of God.

If he talked about faith, he possessed more faith than anyone else. If he taught what it means to pray, no one prayed as he did. If he spoke of loving, it was because he embodied love, his life was the very essence of love.

HIS UNIFIED THEMES

I have been a teacher, have traveled widely, and have written many books; but I am still a humble learner at the feet of the Master. To research this book, I spent months once again reliving the Gospels, listening, reviewing, rethinking. The twelve themes treated in the following chapters are the ones that come up again and again, like golden strands running through Jesus' teachings.

It is only happenstance that there are twelve themes, the number of Jesus' disciples. Or is it? Twelve is a very special number; it is the product of three times four. *Three* is the great dialectical number, and also the number of the Trinity. *Four* denotes wholeness and completeness, as in the four corners of the world and the four evangelists.

One of the interesting things is the way all twelve themes are interrelated. Each has its separate identity, yet is not fully separate, for all the themes tend to merge and become indistinguishable. Perhaps it is because they all proceed from a single source of truth in the mind of

Introduction

God, like the many colors which the poet Shelley said comprise "the white radiance of Eternity."

ONE LAST WORD

This book is no substitute for the Gospels themselves, where one finds the fullest record of the great Teacher in all his glory. But it is my fervent hope that this book will serve as an introduction to the Master's thought and send the reader to the Bible with a new thirst for his words. They are, as the disciples once said, "the words of life."

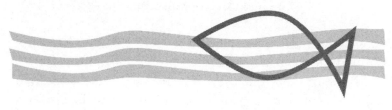

Love

I t has been nearly two thousand years since Jesus lived and taught. Yet the shadow he cast upon the world still grows. And of all his teachings, there is none for which he is better remembered or more revered than those about love.

Even if one knew all the instances of Jesus' influence on this subject, it would be impossible to include all of them in one book. The attempt would require whole libraries. Here are some random samples of this influence:

• **Love in a Prison.** An American woman was touring a government prison in the Philippines. It was a hellhole, she said. Five thousand men were incarcerated behind the thick walls. The only beds were straw mats on concrete floors. For latrines, there were open grooves around the edges of the cells.

As she and the other visitors were escorted through the prison, the prisoners were forced to kneel with their faces against the floor. Suddenly one man reached up, grabbed the woman's hand, and pressed it to his face.

"My heart went out to him," she said, "and I thought of Jesus, with lonely people reaching out to him everywhere he went."

Back in her own country, the woman became active in prison reform work, and even wrote to government officials to see what could be done to improve those prison conditions in the Philippines.

• **Love in a Hospital.** A young man was receiving chemotherapy for cancer. When the treatment caused his hair to fall out, he became very embarrassed by his appearance. He lay all day with his face to the wall and had a "No Visitors" sign put on his door.

But one day that door opened and fifty people—friends, neighbors, and family members—crowded into his room. And all of them had shaved their heads!

It was a turning point, and the young man was no longer ashamed of being bald.

"It's what Jesus would have wanted us to do," said one of the friends.

• **Love Overcoming Fear.** Another man, who had AIDS, was dying in a hospital. His family had abandoned him, and the few friends who did visit occasionally did not stay long. Even many of the nurses did not like to treat the man, fearing for their own safety.

But there was one exception. An older nurse on night duty often stopped to talk with the man, fussed over him, and tried to make him more comfortable.

One night when he was feeling worse than usual, he

told the nurse he didn't want to be alone. Then he asked if she would hold him for a little while, the way his mother did when he was a child.

"Of course," she said, and she climbed onto the bed beside him, held him, and sang lullabies while he died.

"Just like Jesus!" said one of the younger nurses as she stood in the doorway and saw the woman cradling the dead patient.

LOVE—THE CENTER OF EVERYTHING

Love.

It was a strange thing for a man in Jesus' time to be talking about. Most men talked about travel, women, combat, slaves, commerce, agriculture, valiant deeds— not love. Love was a feminine topic, something women talked about.

But Jesus appears never to have been embarrassed to talk about love. It was at the center of who he was, at the heart of his vision. For him, love was always the bottom line—of every interpretation of life, every act of will, every decision involving other persons. Anything that did not proceed from love or answer to love was simply wrong.

The God of the universe, Jesus said, is fatherly— fatherly in the best and warmest sense possible—and this means that it is love, not law, that underlies all God's relationships. People had misunderstood God on this matter. They had assumed, because God had given them the Commandments in the wilderness, that God is hard and restrictive, the way some earthly fathers are. But God isn't that way at all, said Jesus. To his poor and broken children, God is like the father in the story of the prodigal son.

The son in the story was rebellious. He demanded a part of the father's money—the part that would come to him when the father died—to finance a trip abroad. It is amazing that the father gave it to him, for younger sons in that time rarely received any inheritance at all. Yet that father did give it to him. Perhaps he did it with a broken heart, but he did it.

The boy went away, probably as far as he could go, trying to achieve a separate identity. Then when he had fallen on hard times and had learned how lonely and cruel the world can be among those who do not love, he came back. He had gone away proud, boastful, high-spirited. He came back wounded, hurt, humiliated.

But the father loved him and did not gloat over his failure. Instead, the father ran to meet him, embraced him, kissed him, rejoiced over his return. There was no lapse in the father's love. It had continued without a break.

Jesus knew that not everybody understands love. The elder son in the story—the one who had stayed home, where he should have understood the father's love better than anyone—didn't understand. He was jealous, envious, and competitive; and his lack of love was ruining everything—for him, for the father, and for the younger son.

It's always this way in the world. The unloving people ruin things for the loving ones. We see it everywhere. One spiteful child in a classroom creates an atmosphere of distrust and unrest for all the others. A single embittered committee member inclines an entire meeting to confusion and lack of unity. Even a few disgruntled Christians can corrupt the sense of fellowship in a church.

Still, said Jesus, we must try to love. The whole law of life is summed up in love. When asked by a lawyer to state the greatest of the Commandments, Jesus answered without hesitation: " 'You shall love the Lord your God with all your heart, and with all your soul, and with all your mind.' This is the greatest and first commandment. And a second is like it: 'You shall love your neighbor as yourself.' On these two commandments hang all the law and the prophets" (Matt. 22:37-40).

Love—at the center of everything.

LOVE KNOWS NO ENEMIES OR STRANGERS

We should love even our enemies, said Jesus—the very people who misunderstand and betray love. Jesus himself practiced this in the crucible of his final hours, by embracing Judas the betrayer and invoking divine forgiveness for his crucifiers.

Centuries later, this teaching manifested itself in the life of a young African American minister named Martin Luther King, Jr., and affected him so dramatically that he rewrote history on the basis of that teaching. He believed *Strength to Love* to be one of his greatest books. And he did love. He loved a nation so much that some of the people began to forget that they were black or white. And when he suspected that his death was imminent, he said he did not want it noted at his funeral that he had won the Nobel Prize for Peace. He wanted it said instead that he had been a man of love.

Perhaps even more startling than Jesus' demand that we love our enemies was the suggestion that we should love even the people we do not know, people we meet only by chance along life's way.

When someone asked exactly with whom we are to share our lives and substance, Jesus told a story that resulted in an answer that was just the opposite of the questioner's purpose in asking the question. The story showed that *no one* is to be excluded from our love.

The story was about a man who had been severely beaten and robbed by thieves and then left helpless by the road. A priest passed by and did not stop—also a Levite, a member of the tribe of Israelites that assisted the priests in the temple. The two men probably had perfectly legitimate reasons for not wishing to become involved in the victim's plight—perhaps even religious reasons. The very explicit laws that governed their lives may have made it "unwise" for them to help.

Then a Samaritan traveler came along—a man whose people were despised by the Jews. And the Samaritan, wonder of wonders, stopped to assist the man. He not only stopped, but he also took the man to an inn and, out of his own pocket, paid the innkeeper for room and board until the man became strong enough to leave, promising to pay more upon his return, if more were required.

Presumably the man lying half-dead by the road was a Jew, like the priest and the Levite. Of the three passersby, the Samaritan had least reason to stop. He had, in fact, good reason not to stop. Not only did he not know the man, he was a Samaritan. The stranger might spit in his face, disdaining his assistance. Yet he stopped and helped. He showed love to the stranger and thus did what was pleasing to God.

The story has since been told millions of times, in hundreds of languages, as an example of the way all people should live. It has surely altered the very course of human life and philosophy.

A LOVE FOR ALL TIME

The people in Jesus' day who could not understand love, or worse, who lacked the capacity to love others, eventually rose up against him and took his life. His case was not dissimilar to that of the woman of whom Camus wrote—a woman so fine and good that her husband, of a mean and jealous disposition, could not stand her, so one day murdered her.

Jesus knew that his death was coming, that there was no way to avoid it. He tried to prepare his disciples by counseling them to love one another through the time of crisis and beyond. "This is my commandment," he said, "that you love one another as I have loved you. No one has greater love than this, to lay down one's life for one's friends" (John 15:12-13).

Jesus didn't have to die. He could have fought his enemies. Thousands of Jews who had come to Jerusalem for the Passover would have risen to his side, if he had only said the word. But he loved them too much for that. He didn't want any bloodshed. He didn't want a kingdom based on force.

So Jesus went willingly with the soldiers when they came for him; he put out his hands and let them bind him and lead him away. He died on the cross, praying for the forgiveness of the very men who had nailed him there.

Jesus' love has changed the world, and is still changing it. People's lives are transformed through the discovery of his teaching about love.

Toyohiko Kagawa, the great Japanese labor leader, was raised in cruelty and hardship. When he heard about Jesus, he surrendered his life to the Galilean and went to seminary. Even before graduation, Kagawa moved into a tiny apartment in the Shinkawa slums and began to minister to beggars and the sick. At one time he had as many as ten "boarders" in the apartment, necessitating removal of the walls to accommodate all of them. For four years, he slept holding the hand of a murderer, because the man, believing that this would keep away the ghost of his victim, could sleep no other way. One boarder was in the final stages of tuberculosis, and Kagawa washed his germ-infected garments every day.

Once a beggar asked for Kagawa's shirt, saying, "You pose as a Christian; failure to give it to me will prove you a fraud." Kagawa gave him the shirt, and when the man returned the next day and demanded his coat and trousers, he gave him those as well. Observing that Kagawa had nothing to wear, a sympathetic neighbor woman gave him a kimono with flaming red lining, which he wore for a long time wherever he went, making him the butt of many jokes.

 His English biographer, William Axling, said, "He gloried in the belief that Christianity is not a religion of sensible men, but of men gone mad with love for God and man."

One of the most poignant pictures of the influence of Jesus is found in Edward Lewis Wallant's *The Pawnbro-*

Love

ker. The central figure of the novel is an aging Jewish pawnbroker, Sol Nazerman, who lost his entire family in the Nazi death camps and now operates a seedy pawnshop in New York. The crimes and injustices he witnesses every day have begun to revive memories of his suffering in Germany, and he endures horrible flashbacks that leave him weak and confused.

Sol hires an assistant named Jesus Ortiz, a vibrant, irrepressible, ambitious young Puerto Rican. Jesus loves and admires Sol and wants to learn everything about the business so that some day he can take over the store. But Sol is not responsive to Jesus' friendship. He is cynical and rude, maintaining a wall around himself.

Often wounded by Sol's rough refusals of love, Jesus agrees to help two friends rob the pawnshop. They enter the shop disguised in Halloween masks. One of them has a gun and orders Sol to open the safe. When they have emptied the safe and are moving toward the door, Sol indignantly tries to block their way. The man with the gun fires. But Jesus, sensing what is about to happen and caring for the old man, has leaped in front of the gun. As he slumps to the floor, the others flee, leaving Jesus and Sol alone.

Sol removes the mask from the inert form and sees that it is Jesus. He is stunned. For a while, he kneels by the body. Police appear. A crowd gathers. Someone takes word to Jesus' mother, and she comes, sobbing.

Sol stumbles blindly about the shop, overwhelmed by what has happened. The wailing of grief in the room swells in his head, in his entire body. He begins to laugh hysterically.

"*Love?*" he asks himself, unable to comprehend it. "Could this be *love*?"

The whole past—the internment in the camps, the various indignities, the loss of his wife and children—is threaded through the eye of this present moment, and it changes Sol's life. His defenses are knocked down and emotions flood over him, searing and cleansing his psyche. At the end, the reader knows that Sol is a different man. Jesus' loving act, his sacrifice, has saved Sol.

In the film made from the book, in which Rod Steiger played the part of the pawnbroker, there is another touch, a very important touch. When the boy has died, the mother has wept over the body, and the police have finally left, Sol shuffles about the shop like a great bear in excruciating pain. His vision is clouded by tears. Then, as he stands behind the pawn cage, one object on the desk becomes clear in his sight. It is the slender, gleaming spear of a paperspike, rising like a thin obelisk from the clutter of papers.

The pawnbroker stares, his eyes fixed on the paperspike. Then slowly, deliberately, he raises his hand and brings it down on the sharpened end of the spike—down, down, *down,* until he is fully impaled on the shaft of pain. Then he removes his hand, walks out of the shop, and stumbles along the grimy street, returning to life and society.

There is no doubt about the meaning of the gesture. Sol understood the connection between what Jesus Ortiz had done and what Jesus of Nazareth had done, and he sealed the relationship with the image of the crucifixion.

"No one has greater love than this, to lay down one's life for one's friends" (John 15:13).

It is a teaching to live by.

Faith

A few years ago, a conference of noted professors, industrialists, and government leaders was held at Cambridge University. Its purpose was to address the question, "What causes certain persons to become visionaries or achievers in society?" It was hoped that if the participants could isolate the factors that produce such persons, it would be possible to produce more such persons by nurturing those factors in schools and colleges.

The conclusion reached by the people at the conference was very simple: *The greatest visionaries and achievers live as though they are seeing another world.* They live very much in this world, but they appear to have some other world in their sights, and everything they do is governed by that other world.

Such a vision certainly would apply to Jesus, wouldn't it? He was continually in touch with something beyond this world, a vision of the world as belonging to God, and he never wavered from following this vision. Whether he was being tempted by Satan in the wilderness, confronting a religious opponent, or struggling with his own future in the Garden of Gethsemane, he always lived in the grip of this other world.

When he talked about it to his disciples, he called it *faith*. Later, one of his followers would say that faith is "the assurance of things hoped for, the conviction of things not seen" (Heb. 11:1). Nothing could better describe the life of the Master: It was totally surrendered to the service of this unseen world.

As Jesus talked about faith and belief, it became apparent that there are three stages in the way we experience faith, three successive levels of our own surrender to its power.

GOD IS

First, God is. There was not a lot of argument about this belief in Jesus' day, especially in little Israel, which still was perceived by its inhabitants as a theocracy, a country belonging to God. The existence of God was not even considered debatable. As the book of James, which was possibly written by Jesus' brother, says, "Even the demons believe—and shudder" (2:19).

And that is basically true today. Most of us are inherently theistic; we accept the probable existence of a divine being.

I once read of a professor who spent most of a class hour working through a somewhat complicated philosophical proof of the existence of God. In the end, feeling quite pleased with himself, he looked at a student in his class and asked, "Have I proved to you that there is a God?"

"Oh, you didn't have to prove it to me," replied the student, who had not been at all intimidated by the esoteric line of reasoning. "I knew it all the time."

Many of us are like that student. Though we are vaguely aware of scientific explanations for the way the world works—of protons and neutrons and double-helixes and quarks—there is also something in us that accepts, all along, the existence of a higher power. We may not know very much about this higher power, any more than we know about the public transportation system that operates thousands of buses over hundreds of square miles in a city. But just as we see and ride on the buses, and thus accept the existence of that vast and far-flung system, so we have some small, almost negligible experience of God and know that God is, God exists, far beyond our poor powers of discernment and understanding.

Jesus knew that most of the people of his day had faith of this kind, the most elemental kind of faith. But that was not enough, he told his disciples. They must move on to the second stage of faith, to the belief that God cares about them.

GOD CARES

Second, God cares. You must trust this, said Jesus, and thus allay your anxieties about what you shall eat or drink or wear. Behold the prodigality of nature: The birds find food and the lilies are clothed more regally than an ancient king. "If God so clothes the grass of the field, which is alive today and tomorrow is thrown into the oven, will he not much more clothe you—you of little faith?" (Matt. 6:30).

"You of little faith." That was Jesus' constant reprimand of the disciples.

He was in a boat with them when a storm came up. In fact, he was asleep, and it is a sign of his enormous inner calm and confidence that he did not awaken even when the little boat began to toss upon the waves. The disciples were terrified, and they shook him. Almost instantly Jesus rebuked them: "Why are you afraid, you of little faith?" (Matt. 8:26). He calmed the wind and the waves, and the disciples murmured among themselves, saying, "What sort of man is this, that even the winds and the sea obey him?" (Matt. 8:27).

At another time, when the disciples were in a boat before daylight and strong winds came up, Jesus came walking toward them on the water. When they realized it was he and not a ghost, Peter said, "Lord, if it is you, command me to come to you on the water."

Jesus said, "Come." But when Peter was halfway there, he saw the winds whipping up the waves, lost his courage, and began to sink. "Lord, save me," he cried, and Jesus reached out and caught him. "You of little faith," he chided Peter, "why did you doubt?" (Matt. 14:28-32).

These stories are reminders of the way it is with our own faith. It is not hard to have faith, or to think we have it, when there are no particular storms or dangers in our lives. But when troubles come—when the waterpump on the car breaks, when there is illness, when friends desert us, when we lose our jobs—then it is easy to doubt the very existence of God.

Your commitment must be so solid, said Jesus, that you believe even when everything is going wrong. He himself held fast to such belief, even when nailed to a cross. "Father," he prayed as he was dying, "into your hands I commend my spirit" (Luke 23:46).

I remember the night a man drove me to a speaking engagement in a nearby community. It was raining, and the wipers on his Cadillac moved silently back and forth with mesmerizing regularity. As we drove, he told me about his daughter, who had become an alcoholic in junior high school and began taking hard drugs in high school. He had placed her in expensive treatment centers three times; each time, she had gone back on drugs when she was released.

She left home before finishing high school and soon hit bottom in a city several states away, where she received a six-month prison sentence. After a few days in jail, she called and pleaded with her father to come and get her. They would let her go if he would sign for her. Following the advice of an Al-Anon group, he refused. It was the hardest thing he ever did, he said.

Later, after much prayer, he telephoned and asked, "Do you want to come home now?" She said yes, and he drove to the other state and brought her back. "She was so thin," he said, "she didn't even look like my daughter."

After a brief interval, as the wipers traced their relentless journey across the windows, he slowly told about something that had happened while the daughter was in prison. His son and namesake was killed in a motorcycle accident. The police chief, a friend of his, had called him to come and identify the body.

Through the entire narration, the man spoke of what God had meant to him. "Before," he said, "I believed in God. Now I have faith. I couldn't have got through without God."

It was another way of saying, "I moved from merely believing in the existence of God to knowing that he cared for me." Faith became deeply personal.

GOD IS STILL ACTING IN CREATION

Third, God is still acting in creation to bring the world and all his children into harmony with himself. This is the final, highest level of faith Jesus talked about, where believers so completely lose themselves in the hope of the kingdom of God that miracles begin to happen around them. It is a degree of faith that makes many people uncomfortable, for it goes beyond the conventional limits of religious practice. Yet the teaching of Jesus on the subject is incomplete without it.

When you totally align yourself with God, said Jesus, there is no limit to what may happen through the instrumentality of your faith. To a man who had just heard that his daughter had died, Jesus said, "Do not fear. Only believe, and she will be saved" (Luke 8:50).

When the disciples marveled at a fig tree that withered when Jesus cursed it for bearing no fruit, he said, "Have faith in God. Truly I tell you, if you say to this mountain, 'Be taken up and thrown into the sea,' and if you do not doubt in your heart, but believe that what you say will come to pass, it will be done for you" (Mark 11:22-23).

And when the disciples said, "Give us more faith," Jesus replied, "If your faith were as big as a grain of mustard-seed, you could say to this mulberry tree, 'Pull yourself up by the roots and plant yourself in the sea,' and it would obey you!" (Luke 17:6-7 Phillips).

Faith

Now, it is my personal opinion that the Master was not commissioning all his followers to go out and become instant miracle workers, raising the dead, healing the sick, and rearranging the mulberry groves of the world. But he was speaking of the extraordinary power of God, who is still acting to bring his kingdom to birth in this world, and of the incredible things that will happen in our lives and in our vicinities when we surrender ourselves absolutely to this vision.

Sometimes the miracles are quiet and occur almost unnoticed, but they are nevertheless miracles.

Sister Victoria Trujillo, for instance, is in charge of youth and community work for the Roman Catholic archdiocese of Los Angeles. Sister Victoria often becomes impatient with the people she tries to help. "I could not continue," she says, "without the Lord's help."

One day she was working with an immigrant on the many papers he must complete to become a citizen. They had filled out three or four forms, when she produced yet another. The man became angry, shouted at her, rolled all the papers into a ball, and threw them at her.

"I wanted to say 'That's it!'" she said. "But I took a deep breath, said a little prayer, looked at the man, and reminded myself, 'This is the Lord I am doing this for,' and took out some forms and began again."

This, to me, is part of the miracle: God is working to redeem the world, with Sister Victoria working right there beside him, taking the abuse and the hard work for more than thirty years because she has faith in the vision. This is an example of the faith Jesus was talking about—

a faith that keeps us going, a faith that supports us in difficult times, a faith that produces change and renewal in the world.

If we have it, we can never despair—not for long.

In *This Grace Given*, David H. C. Read, the former minister of Madison Avenue Presbyterian Church in New York City, has written of a moment of near despair in 1940, a few months after he and his Scottish battalion had been captured and interned in a Nazi prison camp. Conditions were at their very worst, he said. Letters from home were not getting through. The potatoes, which had been the men's staple diet, had gone rancid. The war news reported great victories for the Nazis.

Read went for a walk around the inside of the wire, and his eye fell on a newspaper with the headline: "LONDON EIN EINZIGES FLAMMENMEER"—"London a Single Sea of Flames"! The news was heart-rending, for his wife was in London.

"Yet," he writes, "a few minutes later, as I stood looking out over the river, I was overcome by an indescribable sense of peace and a strange joy, as if the angels were singing through the barbed wire and reaching deep inside me."

How can we account for this peace and joy at such a moment? There is only one way. It is faith—faith in the God who is still acting in the world, despite wars and hatred and destruction and disease and death and crucifixion, and who will ultimately establish the eternal kingdom on the very campsites of the enemy! Somehow Read knew, despite all the negative signs, that God was still in charge of human destiny.

When Jesus, after his death, appeared to Thomas and

the other disciples in an upper room, Thomas fell down and cried, "My Lord and my God!"

"Have you believed because you have seen me?" said Jesus. "Blessed are those who have not seen and yet have come to believe" (John 20:28-29).

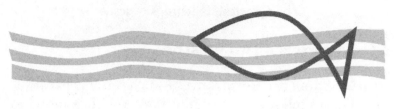

The
Kingdom
of God

Have you ever seen a 3-D movie, the kind in which you wear cardboard glasses that make the images on the screen seem to leap out at you? Viewers duck to avoid avalanches that appear to cascade right off the screen, and shriek as they follow bobsleds down precipitous slopes at breathtaking speeds. In one theater, the realism was so great that when a herd of water buffalo stampeded through a river, the patrons in the first few rows got water in their faces. That is, they did until the manager discovered two small boys crouched under the seats in the front row, discharging their water pistols every time the stampede scene occurred!

The secret of 3-D effects lies in the way the lenses of the glasses unify two different images projected onto the screen. When moviegoers don the special glasses, they are able to see everything from both perspectives at the same time, bringing the objects on the film to life.

LEARNING TO SEE TWO WORLDS

Seeing from two perspectives is, in a sense, what Jesus asked of his followers. Naturally, they would continue to see the world they had always lived in, the world of their senses, the world of politics and society and economics, the world of hard knocks and solid, indisputable facts. But he expected that, at the same time, they should learn to see also the world of God's envisioning—a world of happiness, justice, peace, and sharing, a world where the lion and the lamb can lie side by side in perfect harmony of spirit.

This latter world, he called the *kingdom*—God's kingdom.

An Ancient Teaching

Jesus was not the first to talk about God's kingdom. It had been envisioned as early as the time of Moses, when the law was given to the Hebrews in the wilderness. The law provided for an earthly kingdom in which the strong would care for the weak and the rich for the poor; it even provided for the community's respect and hospitality to be extended to the strangers who entered it. Later, the prophets, that varied assortment of individuals with names such as Isaiah, Jeremiah, Micah, and Hosea, clearly saw the importance of such arrangements and called the people to task for not having lived by them.

Isaiah, in particular, delineated the features of the kingdom of God, dreaming of a time when God would reestablish his people after rescuing them from captivity. "The Spirit of the Lord GOD is upon me," he exulted,

because the LORD has anointed me
to bring good tidings to the afflicted;
    he has sent me to bind up the brokenhearted,
to proclaim liberty to the captives,
    and the opening of the prison to those who are bound;
To proclaim the year of the LORD's favor,
    and the day of vengeance of our God;
    to comfort all who mourn;
    to grant to those who mourn in Zion—
    to give them a garland instead of ashes,
the oil of gladness instead of mourning.

(Isaiah 61:1-3 RSV)

Fulfillment in Jesus

It was a beautiful picture of renewal and restoration, and it was the one with which Jesus identified as he began his own ministry among the people of Israel. Visiting the synagogue in his hometown of Nazareth, he was accorded the honor, often given to guests, of reading the sacred scroll for the day. When handed the scroll of Isaiah, he opened it to these words and read them aloud. Handing the scroll back to the attendant, he sat down. Everyone watched and listened.

"Today," he said, "this scripture has been fulfilled in your hearing" (Luke 4:21).

In what way was the scripture fulfilled? Certainly not by the actual opening of prisons and elimination of suffering; that much is obvious. But Jesus seems to have understood that the spirit of God was upon him to announce the *beginning* of these things. Later, when John the Baptist was imprisoned by Herod and sent his friends to Jesus to ask whether he was the promised

Messiah or they should expect another, Jesus told them, "Go and tell John what you have seen and heard: the blind receive their sight, the lame walk, the lepers are cleansed, the deaf hear, the dead are raised, the poor have good news brought to them" (Luke 7:22). In other words, Jesus saw his ministry as the spearhead of the kingdom—*Jesus' ministry was God's landing on the beachheads of his world, from whence he would eventually produce victory in every place!*

Perhaps today, *kingdom* is not the best word to describe what Jesus was talking about. In his time, everybody understood the word *kingdom,* for the world was ruled by kings. In our time, when the world has far fewer kings, *government* may be a better word. God's *government* will replace the *governments* of the world, and in Christ, God began actively moving toward this final result.

Clearly, God does not govern the world today, any more than God did in Jesus' day. But that did not inhibit Jesus from talking about God's government, or from believing it would one day be complete. When a group of religious people asked when the kingdom of God was coming, Jesus replied, "The kingdom of God is not coming with things that can be observed; nor will they say, 'Look, here it is!' or 'There it is!' For, in fact, the kingdom of God is among you" (Luke 17:20-21).

It is hard to believe that the kingdom of God can coexist with a world of evil and suffering, that it could have been present when Jesus was killed on a cross, or when six million Jews died in Hitler's gas chambers, or when innocent women and children were napalmed in Vietnam; or that it is here today, in a world where there are drug dealers in every grade school, and the elderly are afraid to leave their homes to walk to the supermarket, and terrorists explode bombs in busy department stores and airline terminals. But Jesus was insistent on the kingdom's presence and its mysterious power. The kingdom's beginnings are small and unimpressive, he said, like yeast that a woman puts in the bread dough to make it rise. It is like a mustard seed, he said on one occasion, the tiniest seed imaginable; and when the seed has sprouted and grown, it becomes like a tree, and the birds make their nests in its branches (Mark 4:26-32).

KEEPING FAITH WITH A DREAM

Those who have faith are to live as if they see this kingdom, this government of God, at the same time they are seeing the world as it is. Of course this isn't easy. We are constantly tempted to think the kingdom is only a dream, that it isn't a reality at all. But we are to keep faith with the dream, said Jesus, and never let it go. It is through our faith in the dream that God works in the world.

The great philosopher Immanuel Kant said that all human behavior, all ethics, boils down to a single point: acting "as if" certain things were true. *Als ob* are the German words for "as if." Acting *als ob*—as if Jesus is right, as if the kingdom is a reality, as if God really does govern the world.

And who is to say that the kingdom hasn't come, that it isn't here, when we behave as if it were? This may have been part of what Jesus was trying to teach us: When we see the world through the eyes of the kingdom, the kingdom is actually here in our midst. In other words, the world belongs more truly to God every time we act as if God governs it completely.

I recall a story that James Fifield included in his book *The Silent Path*. During the years after the great stock-market crash of 1929, Dr. Fifield knew a young lawyer named Tom who was having a difficult time supporting his growing family on a rather small salary. Tom's only partner was single, so he got by more easily than Tom. One summer the partner used some of the money he had saved to go to a rather posh hotel for a vacation. A few days after he arrived, he received a check from Tom for one hundred dollars. At last, a paying client had arrived! Where had the client come from? The partner later learned that the client was a relative of Tom's and had called at Tom's house, instead of at the office. If it had not been for Tom's scrupulous honesty, the partner never would have known, for the relative paid Tom in cash.

That extra hundred dollars would have meant a lot to Tom's family just then. The partner, who related the story to Dr. Fifield, confessed that he didn't think he would have reported the income if the roles had been reversed. But Tom's faith was so great, and his commitment to the kingdom so complete, that he could not do otherwise. He lived *as if* the kingdom of God were here among us.

I think of others who live as if the kingdom is among us. A professor and his wife, dear friends of mine, give all his speaking honoraria to various human needs in the Third World and the inner cities of our own country. Their contributions have amounted to thousands of dollars. This couple doesn't have to do this; they could surely use the money for themselves. But they believe that the kingdom of God is in our midst, and they are helping to make it so.

A minister friend tells of a hospice worker who sat one day in his office while she was visiting in his town. She devotes her life to caring for AIDS patients in San Francisco. "As she talked about her work," said my friend, "her face glowed with gentleness and love. When she left my office, I wanted to kneel before her and ask her to bless me." She is only a simple woman behaving as if the kingdom has come, and she makes it so for everyone in her life.

Some years ago I heard about a woman who lived in a small town in the South. Her women's club was voting on the admission of its first black member. Many of the women thought it scandalous even to consider the admission, and they would also exclude anyone who dared to favor the candidate's acceptance. This woman knew what it would mean if she spoke out in behalf of acceptance, and what it probably would mean to her husband's medical practice as well. But she was a Christian, and she had never been able to square the social practices of her community with her belief that, in Christ, there is neither Jew nor Greek, black nor white, male nor female. Therefore she did what she had to do, and found herself, on the day of the vote, making a speech about the kingdom of God to the ladies of her club.

The furor was enormous. The black woman was not accepted, and the woman who made the speech found herself systematically excluded from future luncheons and committees.

But three years later, six women who had belonged to the club came to her and said, "We admire what you did, and we want to start a new club that is open to all women, regardless of race."

This woman had acted as if the kingdom of God were here, and the kingdom gained ground in her town. She lived as if she were seeing the kingdom, and eventually the kingdom became more real for everybody around her.

A DREAM THAT WILL BECOME REAL

"The kingdom of God is in the midst of you"—like tiny seeds that will become a forest of trees, like a prayer that becomes a reality, like a dream that will one day turn into the only world there is. This is what Jesus believed and taught. And when we consider the cross and the impact that the death of one man had on the history of the world, we can believe it too. We can understand why he said that people should seek the kingdom of God more ardently than anything else in life and that, if we do, we won't find ourselves lacking anything for our complete happiness.

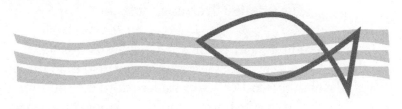

The
Fatherhood
of God

Imagine two great brown eyes, unblinking as two large olives, following a strange man as he moves about the kitchen, opening cabinet doors and setting out food. Orphaned at the age of two and in and out of several foster homes before he was five, the boy is wary and standoffish; he does not know what it is to have a father. Not a father in terms of a man who begot him, but a father who loves and cares, who will nurture and protect and comfort him. He will learn, in time. Relationships must be lived. They can't be forced or rushed. And they can't be summarized in mere words.

This is what Jesus tried to teach his disciples about their heavenly Father. They weren't accustomed to thinking of God as their Father. The august, eternal Spirit who had created the world, had formed a nation from the loins of the elderly Abraham and Sarah, had more than once saved the nation from captivity, and had given the law to Moses in the holy mountain—that very same Spirit was *their Father!*

It was incredible, and yet it was what Jesus was teaching them. Many Jews said it was heresy; worse than that, it was blasphemy. God was too exalted for such humble associations, they said; Jesus should be stoned for suggesting such things, misleading simple folk with blasphemous ideas.

If it was wrong to teach them that God was Abba, their Father, then Jesus was guilty. He taught that they must entrust themselves to God as children to a father, asking him for what they needed, relating to one another as his children, relying on him to care for them, and seeking his guidance in everything they did. If they learned anything from Jesus, it must be this. The whole future of Christianity depended upon it.

A PROBLEMATIC METAPHOR?

Perhaps, as some have suggested, the fatherliness of God was really only a metaphorical way of describing God's nature without limiting God to the characteristics of human fathers. Some fathers, after all, are obviously selfish, brutal, and arrogant, and Jesus surely did not intend that we view God in these terms. And then there is the thought that God has motherly qualities as well and that calling God "Father" may reinforce ancient societal ideas about the superiority of males over females.

Whatever problems there may be with the term, we should not lose sight of the fantastic advancement it gave to the understanding of God as personally caring about us and creating intimate relationships with us. If it is only a metaphor, then it is a radical metaphor indeed, and one beyond which we are never likely to go. God *is* Spirit and can never be fully understood by the finite mind. But when one says "God is our Father" or "God is our Mother," one has done as much as one can to express a true intimacy between ourselves and the supreme God of the universe, the One whom Tillich the theologian called the Ground of All Being.

The real test of any philosophical idea, said Albert Camus, is "how it works in war-time." He had in mind the way war sifts truths, allowing those that are temporary or unimportant to fall away like chaff. The idea of the fatherhood of God certainly came through with flying colors for Jesus in the Garden of Gethsemane. If his understanding of life was ever to fall apart, surely it was there, when D-Day was upon him. The enemy was landing all over his beaches, and the outcome was far from promising. But Jesus never wavered. "Father," he prayed, "if you are willing, remove this cup from me; yet, not my will but yours be done" (Luke 22:42).

Isn't it the same with us?

I remember when, some years ago, I underwent life-threatening surgery. I was a graduate student in literature and philosophy at the time, but I do not remember that I lay in my bed contemplating Aristotelian notions of reality or rehearsing Heidegger's theories of *Existenz.* "O Father," I prayed.

And when my earthly father died and his casket was lowered beside those of my mother and sister, I did not find consolation in thinking of Descartes and Hegel and the great metaphysical tradition in Western thought. No. I cried out, "O Father!"

And when our son had a ruptured appendix, and I

knew there was danger of peritonitis, I did not find myself reflecting calmly on the latest philosophical theories of the nature of life and death. I bowed my head and said, "O Father!"

You see?—God as *personal, intimate, caring.*

Only "Father" or "Mother" can fully bespeak this aspect of God's nature. "I Am That I Am," "The Almighty One," "Divine Creator," "The Holy Other," "Ground of Being"—all are inadequate to express the intimacy of God's nature. This requires a parental noun, the sense of God as *intimately and lovingly related to us.*

ALWAYS SONS AND DAUGHTERS

To say that God is our Father is to define something special about our humanity, something not explained by anthropology alone. It says that we are more than an ingenious aggregate of chemicals and electrical impulses, that we are more than Id and Ego and Super-ego, that we are more than our amazing history of discoveries, inventions, and cultures. We are the children of our heavenly Father and have an ineradicable relationship to him. No matter what we do in life, whether we embezzle from our employers or prostitute our gifts or disgrace our families, we are still the sons and daughters of God and bear the image of our Parent. The image is always there, however hidden or mutilated.

Graham Greene, a Roman Catholic, liked to contemplate this. In his novel *The Power and the Glory,* there is a scene in which a defrocked priest is leading a mule bearing an ugly half-caste with yellow teeth. As the priest walks, he thinks of the question he has been asked so often, "What is God like?" and that he usually has answered it with some reference to a father or mother:

> But at the centre of his own faith there always stood the convincing mystery—that we were made in God's image. God was the parent, but He was also the policeman, the criminal, the priest, the maniac and the judge. Something resembling God dangled from the gibbet or went into odd attitudes before the bullets in a prison yard or contorted itself like a camel in the attitude of sex. He would sit in the confessional and hear the complicated dirty ingenuities which God's image had thought out, and God's image shook now, up and down on the mule's back, with the yellow teeth sticking out over the lower lip.

The image is always there. But not only that, said Jesus, God never disowns it. God is always ready to claim it and renew the relationship. It isn't only the righteous and superrighteous—in his day, the scribes and the Pharisees—who have a right to it, said Jesus. It is also the tax-collectors and prostitutes, the lepers and pariahs; or, to bring it home in our time, the drug-pushers and porno stars, the homeless and criminally insane, and people with AIDS. God is their Father and will not disclaim his paternity.

You see how radical the metaphor really was and why the religious leaders of Jesus' day opposed him, lest his ideas catch on among the people. It is still radical today, of course, and continues to be a thorn in the flesh of the church, which would like to set it aside for its own brand of Pharisaism, preferring a kingdom composed of chaste and respectable men and women who have never smoked marijuana, spoken dirty words, or set a bad example for children.

AN INESCAPABLE METAPHOR

The church can hardly get away from the metaphor, though, especially in view of the immense popularity of Jesus' parable about the prodigal son and his father. The point of that parable is that nothing the prodigal did ever completely destroyed the relationship with his father. First he insulted the relationship by asking for his inheritance early, as if the father had already died. Then he traduced it by living as if all the principles his father stood for were dirt. And finally he treated it as if it did not exist by coming back and trying to hire on at his father's house in a mere business arrangement.

But by none of these methods was he able to obliterate the relationship. It was still intact when the boy came home, and the father's love and generosity overcame not only the distance between them but also the son's own self-loathing and self-destructive tendencies. The relationship held fast, moreover, when the elder son complained about it, denying the prodigal son's right to it. "How can you do this?" he asked. "This son of yours has spent your fortune living with prostitutes, and when he comes back you order the finest dinner to welcome him home!"

This is what Jesus wanted to underline: God always welcomes us home with all his heart. Because God is our Father or Mother, God has an abiding, eternal relationship with us, and it is God's fondest wish to have his wayward children back at his table. However derelict or faithless we have been, we have never once set foot beyond the boundaries of God's love, and God, like the father in Jesus' parable, keeps an eye on the road for every returning prodigal.

A MODERN VERSION OF THE PARABLE

A story I heard as a child has always spoken to my heart. Perhaps, if you have not heard it, it will speak to yours as well. It is about a young man who committed a terrible offense and was sent to prison. His parents were brokenhearted, but the boy wanted nothing to do with them. During his years in prison, he never answered their letters. One letter from his father bore the news of his mother's death, but still he did not answer. When he was released, he traveled from one place to another, getting into various scrapes and occasionally being sent back to prison.

As the years passed and he entered mid-life, the man began to think about home. He became nostalgic, and one day he decided to go back. But what would his father say? All those years, he had not written a word to him. But now at last, he wrote:

Dear Dad,
I'm coming home for a visit. I would like to see you, if you are willing. I will be leaving before you can write me, and will be coming by train. Do you remember how you used to hang a sheet on the big apple tree in the pasture when you wanted the train to stop for the milk cans? If you want to see me, hang a sheet on the tree and I'll get off at the station and come out. If it's not there—well, I'll just keep going.

A few days later, the man was on his way home. The closer to his home the train drew, the more anxious he became. What if his father didn't want to see him? What if his father was dead? What if the apple tree was no longer there? Maybe it had been blown down by a storm and cut up for firewood.

The man approached a priest who was riding in the same car and asked if he could talk. He told about going to prison and disgracing his parents. He admitted he had never written to them. He talked about how much going home meant to him now, and how he feared his father might not see him or might even be dead.

As the train approached his hometown, the man became even more nervous. "There," he said to the priest, "that's the school I used to go to, and over there is the spire of the Lutheran church." But as the train neared the town, he couldn't look any more. He was so worried about whether the sheet would be there, and whether the tree was still there, that he suddenly put his face in his hands and asked the priest if he would look for him.

"Of course I'll do it, my son," said the priest.

"It's just ahead," said the man. "Once we turn this bend, you'll be able to see the old barn and the apple tree. Can you see it? Is the tree still there?"

"Yes," said the priest, "I think I see it up ahead."

"And the sheet," said the man. "The sheet! Is the sheet hanging on the tree?"

The priest laid his hand on the man's shoulder.

"Son," he said, "that old tree's just *covered* with sheets!"

This is what Jesus was saying with his story of the

prodigal son. God isn't some remote power who enjoys our misfortunes and holds us to the bargains we create. God is our Father, and God yearns for our return and reconciliation. The world is his household and he wants peace and joy in it. He wants us to celebrate life together and enjoy what he has made.

Of course, the idea takes some getting used to. We are like the little boy who had to learn what it means to have a father. But once we realize that the eternal God is our Father and wants us to trust him and rely on him for everything, it changes our lives completely. Then we know we are never alone, even in death.

As the song says, "My heavenly Father watches over me."

Judgment

I n the Museum of San Marco in Florence, there is a remarkably vivid painting by Guido di Pietro da Mugello, usually known to us as Fra Angelico, who died in the fifteenth century. It is titled *Il Giudizio Universale—The Universal Judgment* or *Last Judgment*. The upper part of the canvas depicts Christ reigning in heaven, adored by all the saints and angels. Below this heavenly scene the painting is divided into two parts, with crowds of the blessed on the left and crowds of the damned on the right. The blessed are eating and drinking, embracing one another, and generally enjoying themselves. The damned, on the other hand, are clearly suffering. In one group, they are eating one another, and some are even gnawing on their own flesh. Members of another group are simmering in a large vat. The painter obviously was inspired by the biblical text about the separation of the sheep and the goats, with Christ saying to the goats, "You that are accused, depart from me into the eternal fire prepared for the devil and his angels" (Matt. 25:41).

This artist's rendition is one of thousands of such paintings that abound in the museums of Europe and Great Britain, for until recent times the last-judgment scene was considered one of the most important and edifying subjects for an artist. It was graphically depicted in the literature of the Middle Ages, as Dante's *Divine Comedy* so eloquently attests, and repeatedly dealt with in sermons throughout the Christian world, reaching its peak in Jonathan Edwards' thundering oration, "Sinners in the Hands of an Angry God." Edwards was actually a quiet, mild-mannered preacher who kept his head buried in his manuscript as he preached; but his vivid descriptions of suffering in hell moved his hearers to moan and shriek and hurl themselves to the floor.

We are now little inclined to think about such scenes, and ministers in mainline churches rarely if ever devote an entire sermon to the subject of judgment. It is as if the theme belonged to an era of mythology we would all prefer to forget, like those terribly juvenile passages in our early journals, or our first awkward attempts at creating pottery. It is simply "out of fashion" today. If we were editing the scriptures for modern consumption, we would gladly excise the passages that refer to it.

It is amazing, though, if we read the Gospels with a receptive mind, how many times we find Jesus talking about judgment and condemnation. He seems to have spoken of it almost everywhere he went. It was a subject never far from his lips. He condemned the cities that refused to accept his and the disciples' preaching about repentance, saying that even Sodom, the fabled land of wickedness, would fare better in the judgment than they (Matt. 11:20-24). He often berated the Pharisees, who

Judgment

were the leading religious figures of their day, calling them "serpents" and "vipers," and asking how they expected to escape the fires of hell (see esp. Matthew 23).

He told numerous stories about people who were condemned for not receiving God's kingdom, such as the parables of the vineyard (Matt. 21:33-41; Mark 12:1-12); the wedding banquet (Matt. 22:1-14); the foolish maidens (Matt. 25:1-13); the talents (Matt. 25:14-30); the seeds (Mark 4:1-9; Luke 8:4-8), the house built on sand (Luke 6:46-49); and the householder who wouldn't open his home to latecomers (Luke 13:24-30). In Jesus, the Old Testament tradition of *misphat*, or divine judgment on evil, came to its greatest fulfillment; people, cities, or lands that did not surrender to God's righteousness and reconciliation would be destroyed, for God, in the end, must be all in all!

THE TWO SIDES OF JUDGMENT

There are two motifs at work in the biblical idea of judgment. The first is the idea of God's perfection. "Be perfect," Jesus told his disciples, "as your heavenly Father is perfect" (Matt. 5:48). God is the maker, the shaper, the creator of everything, and as the maker, God has the right to destroy anything that does not turn out as he wishes. The prophet Jeremiah said he learned this lesson in the shop of a potter—the potter smashed everything he made that did not turn out well (Jer. 18:1-4).

Peter Karl Fabergé was chief artisan for Czar Nicholas II of Russia. The Fabergé studios produced many of the most exquisite works of art and jewelry the world has ever seen. Fabergé himself was a master craftsman and was unrelenting in his expectations of his employees and apprentices. He kept a thick palette of metal on his desk. Every work that passed through his studio was brought to his desk and carefully examined. If he found even the most minute flaw, he raised his hammer and smashed the item.

This is a picture of the theology of righteousness. We are to be righteous as God is righteous. If we are not, then we are liable to destruction.

The other motif in the biblical idea of judgment is God's love and grace, and his desire to pardon the offender. We see this in God's frequent restoration of the Hebrew people and in Christ's repeated forgiveness of Simon Peter, the disciple who frequently erred and then deserted Jesus at the time of the crucifixion. There is no more tender picture of God's love and grace than in the prophecy of Hosea, where God likens his relationship to Israel to that of a father caring for a child:

> When Israel was a child, I loved him,
>   and out of Egypt I called my son.
> The more I called them,
>   the more they went from me;
> they kept sacrificing to the Baals,
>   and burning incense to idols.
> Yet it was I who taught Ephraim to walk,
>   I took them up in my arms;
>   but they did not know that I healed them.
> I led them with cords of compassion,
>   with the bands of love,
> and I became to them as one
>   who eases the yoke on their jaws,
>   and I bent down to them and fed them.
>   (Hosea 11:1-4 RSV)

Judgment

In other words, God does not really desire the punishment of those who are not perfect as he is perfect. What God wants most is to be reconciled to the offenders, to make peace with his human creatures who have disappointed him. And this is the message of the gospel, the good news that God will receive with affection his wayfaring children, his prodigal sons and daughters, and welcome them back into his eternal household.

It *is* good news, isn't it, to think that what is less than perfect can be loved as much as if it were perfect? There is a Zen Buddhist story about a wealthy man who had always desired the approval of a certain *roshi,* or master. He purchased an incredibly expensive tea caddy, overlaid with the most exquisite filigree of gold, and invited the *roshi* to have tea with him. "At last," he thought, "I shall impress the *roshi* beyond all question!" But when the *roshi* came to tea, he said nothing about the tea caddy. After he left, the man was so angry that he smashed the caddy.

A servant swept up the pieces, carried them home, and painstakingly glued them together. While the result was somewhat less beautiful than the original, the servant was sufficiently proud of his new tea caddy to invite the same *roshi* to join him for tea. When the *roshi* saw the repaired tea caddy, he could not stop praising its great beauty and tastefulness.

I have always liked this story, for it reminds me of the good news of Christ: that God loves us even in our brokenness and imperfection; that in fact, God may even treasure us more because of our imperfections.

But we must be ready to be reconciled to God. The judgment of which Christ spoke so frequently was not upon those who were broken and imperfect, but upon those who would not accept reunion with God when it was offered. God's judgment was upon the Pharisees and the self-contained, and the cities that would not hear the gospel and surrender to a higher sense of community. God's judgment was not upon the tax-collectors and prostitutes and "little people" who had been cast out of the circle of respectability, but upon so-called "good" people who refused to humble themselves before the Almighty.

ADJUSTED NOTIONS OF JUDGMENT

In the modern world, we still believe in judgment, even though we no longer want to hear sermons about hellfire and eternal punishment. We have merely interiorized and temporized judgment. That is, we have come to understand judgment as something that belongs more to our present lives—to the way things are now—than to some future eternal reality. If we do wrong, we expect to suffer for it somewhere along the way in *this* life, not the next. "I'll pay for that," we say to ourselves when we do something we know we shouldn't.

In one sense, we have removed judgment from the arena of spirituality and located it in the region of psychology. Since Freud, we have tended more and more to regard sin as a problem of improper rearing and consequent maladjustment to life. The person who grows up unloved and abused is likely to become a violent adult— even a murderer. That person lives in a kind of hell, shut up within his or her own violent personality. But society at large also suffers, for it must absorb and endure the pain inflicted by the person.

Judgment

Even those of us who view ourselves as rational, well-adjusted individuals regard certain consequences of our thoughts and behavior in terms of an inviolable justice. Karl Menninger, in *Man Against Himself,* said that the person who cuts himself shaving in the morning is probably expiating for some unkind thought or action. We expect to pay for the wrong we do, and when we see ourselves being punished in any way, we tend to think of a connection between that and our weaker, imperfect natures. Thus, in a thousand ways, we still believe in justice and judgment and punishment.

FORGIVENESS AND RECONCILIATION

The good news of Christ is that there is forgiveness, that sinners may be restored to God and wholeness of life, that we need not live with judgment being enacted in our lives and personalities, whether we conceive of it as a present reality or as a future possibility. God does restore us and save us from condemnation.

There is a beautiful picture of this in H. A. Williams' autobiography, *Some Day I'll Find You.* Williams is one of the best known Anglican preachers and theologians of our time. For years he was haunted by an inner sense of frustration and guilt because he is homosexual. A priest, he thought, should not have homosexual feelings. The hidden struggle he endured as a student and as a young minister served to make him unusually sensitive and effective as a preacher, and he was promoted from one respectable post to another. But the inner toll was enormous. He began to hallucinate and experience paralysis. He became terrified of going to public places. His shoes were completely worn out, yet he could not go into a store to buy more. The day came, in his chaplaincy at Cambridge University, when he could not even rise from his bed.

Hospitalization and years of therapy followed, in which he bared to a devoted psychiatrist his sense of guilt and dread, his deep feelings of unworthiness as a priest of God. As a theologian, he understood that the love of God is the most important fact of our existence; but as a sinner, as one under judgment, he believed himself shut off from that love, encased in a wretchedness that prevented its entry. His guilt was choking him, destroying his life.

Eventually, with the help of this psychotherapist, the broken man began to heal. The physical manifestations of anxiety departed; the heart that was filled with terror began to relax and trust again; the mind so tortured fell into tranquility and serene reflection. And most important, Williams began to experience feelings of bliss and reconciliation which came at odd moments, usually for no apparent reason.

One of these blissful experiences occurred when he was in Trinidad on business, traveling by bus from San Fernando to Port of Spain. The trip took two hours, but his sense of ecstasy was so overpowering that he did not notice the passing of time. A feeling of "the ultimate reconciliation of all things as Love, as a living presence," flooded over him, he said, and swept him into its own radiance, combining in itself "an infinite grandeur with a tender personal intimacy." He did not even notice when the bus arrived at its destination until the conductor tapped him on the shoulder and asked if he was all right.

Judgment

Then when he saw that the bus was empty, he thanked the conductor and got out. The experience was so transporting that he walked around the city for half an hour, trying to recover his normal perspective before attending to his business.

Judgment and reconciliation. They are at the heart of the gospel. They are what Christ's teachings were all about. Whether we believe in judgment now or judgment later, we know that it is an inescapable fact of life; and the good news of Christ is that God wants us to be rejoined with him and to be whole again!

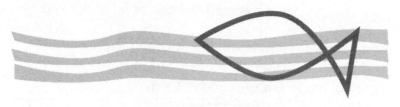

Forgiveness

D o you know what the parents of the Jivaro tribe in Ecuador do? Every night when their children go to bed, they linger by their bedsides and whisper into their ears the names of all the people they must hate when they are older. It is the tribal way of keeping its feuds and enmities alive from generation to generation.

We naturally recoil from such a practice, for we know the hatred and negativity it generates in the unsophisticated minds of children. People are not made to live with such hostility, we say; it corrodes the heart and eats like an acid into the soul. It is not normal to hate in this manner. It is not good for people to live with festering thoughts.

Yet we ourselves are often guilty of such hatred. We resent other members of our families for the way they have treated us. We are jealous of classmates, colleagues, and competitors. We remember moments of hurt or embarrassment, even though they occurred years ago.

Our hearts are warehouses of unsorted wounds, grudges, and disappointments, many of them still capable of bringing fire to our eyes and color to our cheeks.

Some of us nurse a spirit of bitterness all our lives. We overlook in ourselves what we see so easily in the Jivaro children of Ecuador: God did not give us the precious gift of life to squander on feelings of negativity.

FORGIVENESS WITHOUT LIMITS

Jesus taught his disciples to forgive. They were normal human beings, men who came to him with grudges and expressions of unhappiness with others. Peter was probably one of the worst, for he was a volatile man, given to outbursts of tongue and temper. And it was he who strode up to the Master one day and demanded, "Lord, how often shall my brother sin against me, and I forgive him? As many as seven times?" (Matt. 18:21 RSV).

We can imagine the altercation that had precipitated such a question. Perhaps it was with Thomas. Thomas was a quiet, stubborn sort of man who probably had a way of needling others when they offended him. You know the kind—a little dagger here, a little dagger there. Not a lot of bloodletting, but a lot of little stabs. Maybe he called Peter Mr. Know-It-All or Mr. Blabbermouth, for the names would not have been too far from the truth; and it is the accusations with closest proximity to the truth that usually hurt us most deeply, not the insults that miss us by a mile.

Now Peter came with a question, probably offended again and his face red with barely contained anger: "Lord, how many times must I forgive him? He says seven times. Is that true?"

Forgiveness

And Jesus replied, "I do not say to you seven times, but *seventy times seven*" (Matt. 18:22 RSV italics added). It was an impossible number, an astronomical figure, even beyond Peter's imagining. The point was, of course, that there must be no limit to forgiveness. Forgiveness is an attitude, a way of life that grows out of one's understanding of God and the world. The heart that is in tune with the great God produces forgiveness as regularly and effortlessly as the glands of the body secrete the fluids necessary for its harmonious functioning. It is all part of a reciprocal movement of the spirit.

FORGIVENESS MUST BE SHARED

Jesus explained the reciprocity of forgiveness to Peter by telling him the story of the king who was going over his account books and found that one servant owed him a fantastic sum of money, so much that it was impossible for him ever to repay it. Following the usual course in such matters, the king ordered the servant and his family sold into slavery, with the sum they fetched to be applied against the debt. When the man begged for mercy, the king forgave the debt, wiping the slate clean.

Then, on his way out of the court, the man spotted a fellow servant who owed him a comparatively small sum of money and demanded that it be repaid at once. When the servant could not pay, the man had him thrown into prison.

When word got back to the king, he was outraged. He called the man in and fell upon him in a fury. "What do you mean," he said, "treating a fellow servant in that manner, after I forgave you your enormous debt to me!"

And he had the servant taken immediately to prison, to remain there until his original debt should be paid.

"You see," said Jesus, "this is the way it is with you. God has forgiven your sins, as terrible as they were. Now you must share the sense of love and forgiveness with others who have offended you. And whatever anyone has done to you, it cannot begin to compare with the hurt you have caused God."

Some time ago, when I spoke on the subject of forgiveness at a conference of ministers, a minister came to me to confess his hatred for a man. "My wife and I were on a vacation," he said. "When we returned home, there was a note from our daughter. She said she was in prison, but that she had used a false name and we should not try to contact her as her parents. I gained entrance to see her as her minister, and she told me the story. She had been living with a man for a year and a half. We knew she was living with him, but she is twenty-one and there wasn't anything we could do. She told me he is a pimp and she is one of his prostitutes. She made $60,000 for him in a single summer. The police busted her in an undercover operation.

"I went to see this man she had lived with," he said. "I wanted to understand why it all happened. He is from a good family. He is a clever young man. But he was arrogant and nonchalant about it. 'These things happen,' he said. I wanted to strangle him. Now I think about my daughter and the possibility that she will have AIDS. How can I forgive that man? How can I forgive myself?"

I was sympathetic with the great pain he was feeling, for it was obvious in his eyes and voice.

"You are a minister," I said. "You know it is the way of

the world. Jesus said there will always be evil around us; the wheat and the tares grow up together, and we cannot separate them in this life. You must take the long look and remember that God has already forgiven sinners. God has forgiven that man for the awful things he did, and God has forgiven you for the way you feel. Now you must accept that forgiveness as a way of life, and not let your spirit be eaten up by hatred. Otherwise, you will never again be of any help to your daughter, or, for that matter, to the people of your church. You have the opportunity, hard as it may now seem, to live out the gospel of Christ, to make his teachings real in your daily existence."

I have often prayed for the man since the day we talked. I know it is easy for me to see the matter clearly, while he is in pain and confusion. But I am convinced that the teaching of Jesus about forgiveness is true, that it is a matter of the heart we learn from God, who has first forgiven us. This is why Jesus said that we are to pray, "Forgive us our sins, as we forgive those who sin against us." Forgiveness is "all of a piece," and we cannot have our forgiveness without granting it to others.

CUTTING THROUGH THE RED TAPE

As much as anything else, it was Jesus' granting the forgiveness of God that got him into trouble with the religious leaders of his day. Their whole understanding of forgiveness was legalistic—that is, that God will forgive sin when people make the right oblations or perform the right acts of restitution. Under their supervision, the business of sacrificing birds and animals in the temple was prospering, and often the worst offenders purchased a dove, offered it in the temple, and went away lighthearted, satisfied that they had paid off the deity for whatever wrongs they had done. When Jesus forgave the sin of a paralytic or a blind man or a leper and made the person well, the leaders were irate. Only God can forgive sin, they declared, and God does it only through the system!

But Jesus showed us that forgiveness is much more direct and dynamic than that. It is what God wants to give us more than anything else—so much, in fact, that God sent the message with his uniquely begotten Son *as* the message. No system of judicial regulations could ever adequately convey the message; only God's Son could do it.

This is why the apostle Paul, the great theologian of the early church, began his letter to the Christians of Ephesus with a tremendous statement about Jesus as the expression of God's purpose of forgiveness:

> Blessed be the God and Father of our Lord Jesus Christ, who has blessed us in Christ with every spiritual blessing in the heavenly places, just as he chose us in Christ before the foundation of the world to be holy and blameless before him in love. He destined us for adoption as his children through Jesus Christ, according to the good pleasure of his will, to the praise of his glorious grace that he freely bestowed on us in the Beloved. In him we have redemption through his blood, the forgiveness of our trespasses, according to the riches of his grace that he lavished on us. With all wisdom and insight he has made known to us the mystery of his will, according to his good pleasure that he set forth in Christ, as a plan for

the fullness of time, to gather up all things in him, things in heaven and things on earth. (Eph. 1:3-10)

The language is effusive, bubbling, extravagant, for Paul's heart was filled with excitement and praise, but it clearly makes the point: It has always been God's plan for all his children to be united in his love and to live harmoniously among themselves, completely forgiven and forgiving, without hatred or enmity.

PRACTICING WHAT JESUS PREACHED

When we know that we are forgiven, when the realization is internalized and made incarnate, we shall live with joy even among our enemies, and pray, as Jesus did, for the very persons who persecute us. We do not need to be superhuman to do this. We need only remember that God has forgiven us and holds us in the divine heart, and then we can forgive anyone anything, even "seventy times seven."

There is a beautiful example of this in one of the late David Watson's books, *You Are My God*. Watson was the rector of St. Michael's parish in York, England, during the years of its miraculous restitution as a vital fellowship. He and others envisioned having a restaurant and gift shop near the church, which would serve as a Christian meeting place for people who wished to talk about their faith.

The answer to the church's prayers seemed to come in the form of a devoted couple, Philip and Wendy Wharton, who lived in a beautiful home outside of York. Their children were grown and both Philip and Wendy were seeking ways to give more of their time and energy to God. When the church discovered a piece of property almost across the street, the couple agreed to sell their lovely home in the country, buy the expensive building across the street, remodel it, and live upstairs. Wendy would manage the shop and restaurant downstairs.

Everyone was overjoyed and felt God's leadership in the project. The Whartons sold their home and moved in with friends while the restaurant and shop were being remodeled. It was decided that the restaurant would be known as The Mustard Seed, indicating the hope that it would develop from small beginnings into a ministry of great influence.

For a while, everything went well. Many people came to The Mustard Seed and always commented on the wonderful atmosphere of the place and how much better they felt just being there.

Then some tensions developed in the membership of the church, and The Mustard Seed was involved in the ensuing conflict. Some people felt that Wendy's ministry was becoming too evangelistic. Contention snowballed, as it often does, and the leadership of the church decided that The Mustard Seed should be abandoned. The Whartons were caught in the crossfire. They lost a great deal of money in the closing of the restaurant and sale of the property. Although they were able to continue living in the apartment above the shop for another two years, they then had to move and buy a tiny house elsewhere. We can imagine how deeply they were wounded.

Yet David Watson wrote: "It was nothing less than a miracle of God's grace that they were eventually able to forgive, and once again became active members of the church which had hurt them so much."

He did not say how the Whartons managed it, only that they did. We are left to imagine the slow recovery from grief, the sorting out of bitter remarks, the assessment of losses, the hours of prayer and meditation, the remembrance of Christ's sufferings, the study of his teaching on forgiveness, the eventual decision that they too must forgive those who had hurt them, and finally, the reunion with the church.

Life is painful. There will always be injuries. But we must never forget that God has forgiven us all in Christ, and that, as Paul said, God wants "to gather up all things in him, things in heaven and things on earth." In that way, we transcend the pain and the pettiness, and find life and peace and joy.

In the end, that is the only way.

Prayer

A friend told me about a woman he met in the parking lot of a local bookstore. She had a great bundle of books in her arms. "What in the world are you doing?" he asked. "Are you opening your own bookstore?"

"No," said the woman, "all these books are about prayer. All my life I have been hearing about the importance of prayer, so I finally decided to learn how to pray. I have bought fourteen books on the subject. And not only that, I have signed up for two courses in prayer, one at my church and one at a friend's church. I am really going to master this subject!"

Several weeks later, the friend ran into the woman again, this time at the grocery. "How is the big project going?" he asked. "Have you learned to pray?"

She hung her head and made a gesture of despair. "It was too complicated," she said, "and I gave it up. Now I'm taking a course in yoga."

There *are* a lot of books on prayer, expressing many

differing viewpoints, and there are also a lot of courses on prayer. But the four Gospels are still our best guide to the understanding of prayer, and what we find in the teachings of Jesus is not really very complicated.

Jesus himself was clearly a man of prayer. He lived in constant communication with his heavenly Parent. Prayer was as natural to him as eating or breathing or sleeping, and sometimes, as we see in the Gospels, he neglected eating and sleeping in order to pray.

Karl Menninger, in *Man Against Himself,* quotes from the diary of Father William Doyle of the Society of Jesus, a chaplain killed in Europe in 1917:

> I long to get back to my little room at night to calm and quiet, and yet I dread it, for He is often so loving there. . . . It is such a helpless feeling to be tossed about, as it were, on the waves of love, to feel the ardent, burning love of His heart, to know He asks for love, and then to realize one human heart is so tiny.

Jesus must have known this mystical, compelling side of prayer, for it drew him aside sometimes for weeks at a time. It drove his life, the way an engine drives a ship, and kept him going in his ministry when a person with less motivation might have abandoned everything, including his unimaginative followers.

THE MODEL PRAYER, OR LORD'S PRAYER

Jesus' followers were obviously impressed by the power of prayer in his life, for they begged him to teach them to pray as he did. On one occasion when they asked this, he gave them the simple words of what we now call the Lord's Prayer:

Prayer

Our Father who art in heaven,
Hallowed be thy name.
Thy kingdom come,
Thy will be done,
On earth as it is in heaven.
Give us this day our daily bread;
And forgive us our debts,
As we also have forgiven our debtors;
And lead us not into temptation,
But deliver us from evil.
(Matt. 6:9-13 RSV)

Liturgical usage eventually led to the adding of the familiar conclusion: "For thine is the kingdom and the power and the glory, forever. Amen."

It is a short prayer—only fifty-seven words in the Greek—yet it contains the very essence of Jesus' life and teachings: God as the Father, worthy of all honor; the importance of the kingdom, even now at the door, which will turn earth into a heaven where the divine will is constantly done; an awareness of the minimal needs, daily bread; a request for general amnesty from sins and offenses, that should characterize the new society; and a desire not to fall away from faith and be plunged back into darkness and confusion. As I have indicated more fully in *The God Named Hallowed: The Lord's Prayer for Today*, this is a prayer around which we should all form our lives, so that we become true sons and daughters of God.

WHAT WE SHOULD PRAY FOR

But this so-called Lord's Prayer was only a small part of what Jesus taught his disciples about prayer. The

75

Gospels are peppered with references to prayer and praying, and we should also attempt an overview of the teachings covered by these references. Basically, Jesus taught his disciples to pray for five things.

The Presence of God

First, Jesus taught his followers to pray for the presence of God. Even if they did not specifically ask for that presence, they were to seek it by going apart when they prayed. Again and again, we find references to Jesus taking the disciples aside to a wilderness place, to the mountains, or to the sea, where they could concentrate on communing with God. When he and the disciples retreated to the Garden of Gethsemane the night before he was crucified, it was, as Luke notes in his Gospel, their custom to do this. Every evening after dinner, apparently, they went as a group to some quiet place to be alone with God.

The "listening prayer" one hears so much about today is an outgrowth of this kind of praying. Whether done in a great cathedral or in a place in the woods or in a quiet place at home, the sense of the divine presence is deliberately cultivated. Such prayer drives out the alien spirits of the marketplace and quiets the voice of selfish interest, so that the beautiful, generous Spirit of God can take over and work its profound changes on the personality of the one praying.

The old hymn "In the Garden" expresses it simply and poetically:

> I come to the garden alone
> while the dew is still on the roses,

Prayer

and the voice I hear falling on my ear,
The Son of God discloses.

And he walks with me,
and he talks with me,
and he tells me I am his own;
and the joy we share
as we tarry there,
none other has ever known.

Henri Nouwen speaks in his book *Gracias!* of the effect of regularly putting himself in the presence of God while he resided at a Carmelite monastery. It was not always a singularly inspiring time, he said, for often there were distractions, and he was sometimes sleepy or inattentive. Yet the cumulative result in his life was quite noticeable, and he sometimes has a great longing to go back to the chapel:

Yes, I notice, maybe only retrospectively, that my days and weeks are different days and weeks when they are held together by these regular "useless" times. God is greater than my senses, greater than my thoughts, greater than my heart. I do believe that he touches me in places that are unknown even to myself. I seldom can point directly to these places; but when I feel this inner pull to return again to that hidden hour of prayer, I realize that something is happening that is so deep that it becomes like the riverbed through which the waters can safely flow and find their way to the open sea.

Our lives are deepened and enriched by the presence. There is nothing else like it in all the universe.

The Greatest Teachings of Jesus

The Kingdom of God

Second, Jesus taught his disciples to pray for the coming of the kingdom of God and for their personal commitment to it. They understood the kingdom of God—life thoroughly transmuted by the arrival of the deity—through prayer. So do we. You cannot dwell in the presence of the Almighty One for a period of time each day and not begin to comprehend that life could be quite different if everyone felt what you feel. As your desires are changed, as the divine love washes over your soul, as you feel caught up in the tides of eternity and new life, you see the whole world differently.

If only everyone saw the world this way, you suspect, there would be no more war, no more poverty, no more injustice. God's rule would become the most important thing in the universe. God's will would be done on earth as it is in heaven. This is what the kingdom is, you see, viewing the world as God views it. And you cannot see this regularly without becoming personally committed to it.

I remember the occasion when I approached a man about helping with a certain program in a church. "Oh, I don't have time for that," he said. "I am very busy."

"I understand how busy you are," I replied, "but would you be willing to come and meet with our committee for only an hour after church one Sunday, and give us the benefit of your insights and understanding?" And he finally agreed to do this.

The upshot of it was that, having spent an hour, he became interested enough to come back the following week, and by then he was so involved intellectually and emotionally in what we were undertaking that he became a leader in the program.

This is the way it is with the kingdom. When we wait in the divine presence and seek the kingdom's appearance, our own lives are invariably drawn into the kingdom's program. We cannot avoid it.

Personal Needs

Third, Jesus instructed the disciples to pray for whatever they needed—always, of course, in light of their experience of the presence and kingdom of God. It is important to remember the presence and kingdom of God, for without these, one might think that Jesus assured the disciples that their prayers for anything would be answered.

He said, "Ask, and it will be given you; search, and you will find; knock, and the door will be opened for you. For everyone who asks receives, and everyone who searches finds, and for everyone who knocks, the door will be opened" (Matt. 7:7-8). He also said, "Have faith in God. Truly I tell you, if you say to this mountain, 'Be taken up and thrown into the sea,' and if you do not doubt in your heart, but believe that what you say will come to pass, it will be done for you. So I tell you, whatever you ask for in prayer, believe that you have received it, and it will be yours" (Mark 11:22-24). And he told a parable about a widow who petitioned a judge until the judge finally decided in her favor (Luke 18:1-8). This suggests that God will respond to us if we are persistent in seeking what we want.

But the whole matter of asking God for what we want

takes on a different color when we set it in the context of the changes that are wrought in our lives and desires as we spend time daily in the presence of God. Like the alcoholic who no longer wants a drink or the thief who is appalled at the thought of stealing, we find ourselves no longer asking for things we once wanted. Instead, we make our petition for food for the hungry and healing for the sick, for strength for the weak and peace for the troubled. In short, we pray for kingdom conditions for everybody and find ourselves in very little need.

More and more, we find ourselves praying like the little girl whose parents stopped outside her door when they saw her on her knees. As the parents listened, they heard her saying her ABCs: "A-B-C-D-E . . . "

"Dear," said the mother, "we thought you were praying."

"Oh, I was," she answered perkily. "But God knows everything I need, so I just say the alphabet and let him make up my prayers out of the letters."

Eternal Life

Fourth, Jesus taught his followers to pray that after death they would be gathered up by God into the eternal community. In the great "shepherd's prayer" in John 17, when Jesus was praying for the disciples at their last supper, he asked repeatedly that they be kept in God's hand and brought safely through the trials that lay ahead of them. The following day, as he was hanging on the cross, the disciple who was closest to him heard Jesus' final words: "Father, into thy hands I commend my spirit!" (Luke 23:46). He must have given them this lesson constantly: The God who is able to keep us in life is able also to preserve us in death.

Doctors, psychologists, and ministers—those who deal with many people and have the opportunity to observe how they live—often note that those who are happiest and healthiest are those whose deep, abiding faith in God assures them of their personal security, both in life and in whatever state they find themselves after life. Ironically, of the two people who work late in a large office building, one a cleaning woman and the other a wealthy employer, it may well be that the cleaning woman, with her simple faith in God and uncluttered way of life, is far better off than the employer, whose unceasing busyness and frustrations are robbing him of all personal joy.

More than a quarter of a century later, I still have a vivid memory of dear old Mother Crossley, an invalid I visited regularly when I was a pastor in a northern church. Coming to this country from England as a young bride, Mother Crossley had been a midwife; she had delivered more than five thousand babies! In her later years she had developed a large inoperable tumor and spent the remainder of her life in bed and in a wheelchair, confined to her room.

Her son and his wife were members of our parish, so I went every week to see Mother Crossley. She was often in great pain and could not help groaning with discomfort, but she was cheerful and thoughtful of her visitors, and I never left her room without having received a blessing.

Sometimes when I slipped quietly up the stairs, Mother Crossley would not hear my approach, and I would stand outside her door a moment, listening to her prayers. Many times, I heard her say, "Take me home, Lord, take me home. I'm a burden to everybody. Take me home."

At the end of a long and productive life, she knew how to pray the prayer that Jesus had taught the disciples. She wanted to be gathered up in God with all the saints.

Our Enemies

Now, that might seem to round out Jesus' teachings on prayer. *But there was one more thing he taught the disciples to pray for: their enemies.* This was the kind of praying that brought everything full circle.

First they had prayed for God's presence, transforming their lives and wills. Then they prayed for the kingdom and their commitment to it. Next they asked for whatever they needed, in light of the presence and the kingdom. And then they prayed to be kept in God's love, both in life and in death.

But there was something missing that still needed to be gathered up in prayer—their enemies, the people who misused them, were unfriendly to them, or even persecuted them. These people alone stood outside the circle of the life they had discovered in God. It was necessary, said Jesus, to pray for them and thus enclose them in the circle too. So he said to the disciples:

> You have heard that it was said, "You shall love your neighbor and hate your enemy." But I say to you, Love your enemies and pray for those who persecute you, so that you may be children of your Father in heaven; for he makes his sun rise on the evil and on the good, and sends rain on the righteous and on the unrighteous.

Prayer

For if you love those who love you, what reward do you have? Do not even the tax collectors do the same? And if you greet only your brothers and sisters, what more are you doing than others? Do not even the Gentiles do the same? Be perfect, therefore, as your heavenly Father is perfect. (Matt. 5:43-48)

It is important to be perfect—to go full circle—taking in everything and everybody, including the whole world, in your faith.

It wasn't enough for the disciples to have faith by themselves. As God sought reconciliation with all his creatures, so they too must desire it and pray for it, regardless of how they felt about their enemies. And the amazing thing, which they doubtless discovered as they prayed for their enemies, was that *they had no enemies!* An enemy one prays for is no longer a real enemy.

Once when I was on an airplane, I had my notepad and New Testament open on the tray table in front of me, preparing a sermon I was scheduled to give. The man sitting beside me said, "Pardon me, are you a reverend?" I smiled and acknowledged that I was.

"I want to tell you something," he said, pointing to the New Testament. "That book knows what it's talking about. I mean, about forgiving your enemies."

It seems that the man had been engaged to the daughter of his employer. Then a new man, a smooth talker and snappy dresser, was taken into the firm, and soon had worked his way into the daughter's affections. When the daughter married the new man, he was made manager of the section in which the other man worked.

"Was I mad!" said the man. "I was so consumed with anger that I couldn't stand to work there anymore, and I quit. I hated that man. He had deprived me of everything I cared about. If I ever wished anybody dead, it was him!"

The man took a position with another firm, moved up in the company, eventually married another girl, and had a family. His hatred for the other man, strong as it was, was temporarily forgotten.

Then one day when two new employees were assigned to the man's division, he learned that one of them was his old enemy, and the festering hatred broke loose inside him, spilling its poison everywhere. "Every time I looked at him," said the man, "I thought of how he had taken everything that would have been mine, and I despised him. It was so bad, I thought I would either kill him or go crazy."

"How did he react to you as his superior?" I asked.

"That was the worst part," said the man. "He didn't seem to mind at all that the roles were reversed and he was working for me. He was as pleasant and friendly as he could be. So I couldn't just fight with him and have him demoted. It would have made me look terrible!"

"So what happened?" I asked.

"Finally," he said, "it got so bad I went to my priest. I'm a Catholic. I told him I was either going to kill the guy or go crazy. The priest said, 'Do you remember my homily last week?' I made some excuse, because I hadn't been in church. 'It was about Jesus dying on the cross,' he said, 'and how he looked down as he was dying and saw the religious leaders who had insisted on his death and the soldiers who had crucified him, and he prayed for them, asking God to forgive them because they didn't really know what they were doing.' "

"Bingo!" the man continued. "It went on in my head like a light! If Jesus could pray for those guys who did that to him, then I could pray for this man who had screwed up my life. And so I did. It wasn't easy at first. Matter of fact, it was probably the hardest thing I ever did. But I did it. And you know what?" By this time, his voice was getting louder and he was very excited.

"We actually became friends, this guy and me. We get our families together once or twice a month. He and I go out together. We even laugh and talk about the old times, when we first started working together. Sometimes I even thank him for taking my girl away from me, because I think I got a better deal in the one I married. It's a miracle," he said. "That book really knows what it's talking about!"

I think it does too.

Jesus understood what life is all about, and how to get the most out of it. And that is why he taught the disciples to pray as he did.

Custodianship

A friend of mine is a highly skilled engineer, and his company once sent him and his wife to live temporarily in Paris, whence he was able to travel easily to jobs all over Europe. When the couple left their home on Long Island, they were pleased to place it in the care of a middle-aged woman who had excellent references and promised to look after it as if it were her own.

Indeed, she did look after it as if it were her own. When she grew tired of the color of the kitchen, she repainted it to suit herself. When she decided she didn't like the wallpaper, she took a can of paint and redesigned it to her own taste. When the thought struck her that the exposed beams on the ceiling did not appear old enough, she took a hatchet and proceeded to "age" them. And when my friends' tour of duty was ended and they returned to the States to reclaim their home, she had become so convinced it was hers that she refused to leave. A court order and a sheriff were necessary to remove her!

"The nerve!" we say. "How would anyone have the gall to behave that way about property that was not hers?"

Yet this is precisely the point of Jesus' story about the vineyard. The owner of the vineyard left it in the care of tenants who forgot who it belonged to. Three times the owner sent servants to collect his profits from the vineyard, and each time the tenants beat the servants and sent them away. Finally the owner sent his son to collect, thinking surely they would not treat his son that way. But when the tenants saw the son, they thought, "The old man must be dead, and now his son is trying to collect. If we dispose of him, the vineyard will be ours and nobody will know the difference." So they killed the son (Luke 20:9-15).

CARELESS CUSTODIANS: A RECURRING THEME

We would like to think that Jesus was talking about Israel and its rejection of the Messiah. Perhaps, at one level, he was. But the context in the Gospel of Luke suggests that there are other levels of the story as well. In fact, there is hardly a chapter of the Gospel, from the midpoint on, that does not contain a reference to the way we all tend to forget who the earth belongs to and how we ought to live on it.

First, in chapter 12, there is Jesus' story of the rich man whose crops grew in such abundance that he was preparing to build great storage barns to hold them, and then live the rest of his life in ease and luxury. But suddenly his heart gave out and he died. Then God said, "Now whose will these things be?" (16-21).

In chapter 15 is the story of the young man who asked

for his inheritance early, took it abroad, and lost everything. Fortunately, the story has a happy ending, up to a point, for the young man finally sees the light and returns to his father's house (12-24).

In chapter 16 there are two stories—one is about a wicked custodian who realizes his master is about to cast him out of the house, and so he scurries about, making amends as fast as he can; the other is about a rich man who dies and wakes up in hell because he neglected the poor sick man who lay at his gate begging alms (1-9, 19-33).

In chapter 17, Jesus talks about uppity servants who come into the house after plowing or keeping sheep and expect the owner of the farm to prepare a hot meal for them. Jesus asks whether the owner would not say to the servants, "Prepare supper for me, put on your apron and serve me while I eat and drink; later you may eat and drink" (7-10). Jesus speaks, we suspect, about those of us who forget our station with God and expect him to treat us more royally than we deserve.

In chapter 19 is the story of the pounds, known in Matthew's Gospel as the parable of the talents (Matt. 25:14-30). A nobleman takes a long journey, and while he is away, he entrusts ten servants with a pound apiece, saying, "Do business with these until I come back." When he returns, he calls in the servants to see what they have done with his money. One has turned the single pound into ten, and is praised. Another has turned the pound into five, and is likewise commended. But one of the ten has done nothing with his pound but hide it in a napkin, and the master is so angry that he takes the pound away from him and gives it to the man who turned his pound into ten (Luke 19:11-27).

Finally, after the story of the vineyard in chapter 20, there is an unexpected positive note—I say "unexpected," for all the other examples have been negative. In chapter 21, Jesus was sitting by the temple treasury, watching people bring their gifts, when he was struck by the sight of a widow putting in two copper coins. "Truly I tell you," he said to the disciples, "this poor widow has put in more than all of them; for all of them have contributed out of their abundance, but she out of her poverty put in all she had to live on" (Luke 21:1-4).

The story of the vineyard, you see, was no passing thought with Jesus, and it probably was not intended to speak of Israel alone. Everywhere he looked, Jesus saw people who were greedy, selfish, and avaricious, people who forgot that God owns the world, that all of us are his servants, who should live sensitively, caringly, and generously with all his other servants.

MIXED-UP PRIORITIES

Jesus would see the same thing today, wouldn't he, if he were to walk in our midst? He would see people who think their nice houses and automobiles belong to them; who believe their jewelry and bank accounts and CDs are theirs alone; who forget that their stocks and bonds, their investments in businesses and apartment houses, are really God's, not their own; who live without concern for the poor and hungry or for the victims of war in small countries on the other side of the globe; who turn a blind eye to the way we are despoiling the lakes and seas and polluting the atmosphere, without remembering that they are a trust from God for future generations.

Custodianship

What failures we are as royal custodians!

We erect beautiful homes for ourselves and curse the government when it erects hovels for the poor.

We pay astronomical salaries to TV stars, athletes, and executives, and almost nothing to those who teach our children.

We indulge ourselves in $30 meals and $500 suits and $25,000 automobiles, and give $5 a week to the church.

We spend millions on banks and insurance companies and corporation headquarters, and make the churches and colleges and charitable organizations beg for a pittance.

It's all backward, isn't it? Our priorities are turned upside down; the scale of values is confused.

Archbishop William Temple once said that it's as if a prankster had slipped into the store window at night and mixed up all the pricetags, so that a pair of roller skates costs $5,000 and a fur coat is only $1.98. Having forgotten that the earth is the Lord's, and the fullness thereof, we don't know what is worth what. We teach our children to work sixty hours a week for financial security and prestige in the community, and we don't care if they forget how to be loving and tender toward one another. We erect enormous buildings for our financial and scientific institutions, while we permit many churches and synagogues to fall to rack and ruin for lack of funds. We say we believe in God, but many of the things we do proclaim our belief in earthly security and self-indulgence.

LIVING AS PROPER TENANTS

"Do not store up for yourselves treasures on earth," said Jesus, "where moth and rust consume and where thieves break in and steal; but store up for yourselves treasures in heaven, where neither moth nor rust consumes and where thieves do not break in and steal. For where your treasure is, there your heart will be also" (Matt. 6:19-21).

That's the secret, isn't it? Where the treasure is, the heart follows. If our treasure is in earthly things, our hearts are imprisoned in the earth, and we forget our custodianship, we forget that the whole earth belongs to God. It is when we remember *whose* we are and *whose* the earth is that our hearts are able to soar and life becomes truly beautiful.

Wouldn't it be wonderful if nothing in the earth belonged to anyone who did not remember that it is God's and use it accordingly? It would solve all our problems of property ownership, food distribution, medical help, and education for the masses. If only nothing belonged to anyone who did not acknowledge God's true ownership, our world would function as a paradise!

Jesus knew the world would never work this way, not short of some apocalyptic reversal, at any rate; but he did require of his followers that they—*we*—behave as if everything belongs to God. We are not responsible for the actions of the rest of the people of the world, only for our own. We are to remember *our* custodianship and to live as proper tenants, giving glory to the real owner of everything.

HANDLING EVERYTHING AS IF IT WERE GOD'S

A friend told me about a minister who was visited by a young couple whose aunt had recently died. When the aunt's will was read, the couple learned they had inherited $1.5 million. They were stunned, for they had no idea the aunt had so much money.

"This fortune is destroying us," they said to the minister. "We used to enjoy life enormously. We are simple people with simple tastes. Now we have all this money, and it's worrying us to death. What should we do with it?"

"Give it away," said the minister.

"But we can't do that," said the couple.

"You said it's destroying you. You should give it away." So they agreed to go and pray about it.

A week later, they went to the minister and said, "You're right. We have prayed about the money and we have decided to give it away. We have drawn up a list of worthy causes we would consider giving it to, and we would like you to look over the list and give us your opinion."

The minister took the list and looked at it. "These are all wonderful causes," he said. "I know most of them and think quite highly of them. But you should keep the money."

"What was that?" they asked.

"I said, 'You should keep the money.' "

"But you said we should give it away."

"Ah, yes," said the minister, "that was when you thought the money was yours. Now that you know it isn't, you should keep it and use it. If you give it all away, it will help the recipients right now. But if you take care of it and act as stewards of it for God, it will go much further and bless more people in the long run."

The person who told me this story said, "I am telling

you this because it has changed my life. I now understand what it means to be a steward of the things that
belong to God. It means that I am responsible for them
all the time. I can't merely give them away and be done
with it. I have to handle everything every day as if it is
God's."

"Handle everything every day as if it is God's." That's
what Jesus was trying to teach his disciples. It is what he
would like to teach us. And if we learn it, we will be like
the prudent servant in the parable who heard his master
say, "Well done, good and faithful servant; you have been
faithful over a little, I will set you over much; enter into
the joy of your master" (Matt. 25:21, 23 RSV).

Service

I t was just like a concerned mother—or father, for that matter. Her two sons, James and John, had been in training for months under a famous rabbi. There was even talk that this rabbi, whose reputation for healing and other miracles was widespread, was the long-awaited Messiah of Israel. Now he was on his way to Jerusalem for the high holy days. The sons, telling their mother good-bye, hinted that things were intensifying, that their Master was even speaking of the arrival of the kingdom of God. She did the most natural thing a mother would do. She came to Jesus, fell down before him, and asked a favor.

"What do you want?" asked Jesus.

"Command that these two sons of mine," she said, "may sit, one at your right hand and one at your left, in your kingdom" (Matt. 20:21 RSV).

She had her ideas of greatness for her boys. What parent doesn't blush at the recollection of similar ambitions for a child?

"My daughter really deserves to be in the honors program. She is one of the smartest girls in her class."

"My son would make a first-rate assistant in your shop. He is very bright and a hard worker."

"My daughter would contribute much to your company. She graduated at the top of her class."

"My son would very much like to get into your medical school."

"If you will just give my child a chance, you will not regret it."

Jesus' answer had two parts. First, the mother did not know what she was asking: His kingdom would be reached by way of a cross. Second, anybody who really wants to be great must be the servant of all. Later we will consider the first part. For now, let's think about the second part—being great by serving.

GREATNESS THROUGH SERVICE

If you would go up, said Jesus, you must go down. Anyone who goes down, who willingly becomes the servant of others, goes up. It is a set of directions the world has trouble learning.

In a recent television interview, a psychologist was discussing a survey she had made of the beliefs and attitudes of 287 college-age young people. She was dismayed at what she learned. Almost all the young people, she said, wanted either greatness or satisfaction out of life; yet few of them understood that there was any connection between being great and serving others. "They are a generation accustomed to being served," concluded the psychologist, "not to serving."

Service

Our society has a way of separating greatness and serving. A friend who had conducted a personal survey of the ten top business people he knows, all C.E.O.s of banks, insurance companies, and various industries, reported that none ever makes or serves coffee, none ever sharpens a pencil, none ever operates a vacuum cleaner, only one ever writes a letter for himself, and only six drive themselves to work (the other four have chauffeurs).

A minister once wrote a sermon called "Care and the Uppity Woman," in which she suggested that one reason politicians are so ready to start or prolong wars is that they are so far removed from the direct line of serving others. If they only had the care of small children—feeding, diapering, and bathing—she argued, they would not be so ready to commit them to battle.

Even the church, the institution most committed to service, ironically separates its top personnel from the most direct forms of serving. I cannot recall how many times over the years I have started to do some mundane thing around the church building, only to have a lay person intervene and say, "Here, let me do that. You're the minister and shouldn't have to do that."

Søren Kierkegaard, the Danish philosopher, once observed that the more eloquently a minister speaks about suffering, the finer becomes that minister's carriage and the more removed that minister becomes from suffering.

There is a story about a wise old minister who was visiting a great church. He asked an usher if he might meet the person responsible for the church. The usher took him to the pastor of the church. "No," said the old minister, "this is not the person." The usher took him to meet the chairman of the board. "No," said the minister, "this is not the person." Scratching his head, the usher led him to the wealthiest person in the church. "No," said the minister, "this is not the person I am seeking. Please take me to the kitchen."

The usher, puzzled, led the old man to the kitchen, where a modestly dressed woman in an apron stood at the sink, her arms plunged among dirty coffee cups and saucers. "Here, my friend," said the old minister to the usher, "is the real secret of your success. I have seen it in church after church. Jesus said, 'If any person will be great, let that person become the servant of all.' "

The Lord as Role Model

By word and example, Jesus frequently extolled the importance of humble service. On the final night of his life, when the disciples in the upper room were arguing among themselves about who was greatest, Jesus took a towel, tucked up the ends of his robe, and commenced to wash their feet, a task normally left to slaves or servants. He told them: "If I, your Lord and Teacher, have washed your feet, you also ought to wash one another's feet" (John 13:14).

Great Servants of Yesterday and Today

The truly great persons of the ages have been those who reflected this Christlike humility in their service to others. Francis of Assisi, Florence Nightingale, Albert Schweitzer, Gandhi, Mother Teresa—their names shine above even those of Plato, William Shakespeare, and Albert Einstein. One inevitably has the feeling that if all these famous persons met in the afterlife, the latter would immediately bow down to the former.

We know from the teachings of Jesus that giving a cup of cool water to a thirsty creature is more important in the eyes of God than earning $50 million or writing a beautiful sonnet. Walt Whitman, the poet, is surely more celebrated in heaven for nursing Union soldiers during the Civil War than for writing the poetry in *Leaves of Grass*.

I reflect on Mother Teresa and her ministry to "the lowest of the low and the poorest of the poor." How tirelessly this little nun, scarcely five feet tall, has labored to bring comfort and love to the poor, to save the lives of lepers, to rescue unwanted children from dustbins and see them placed with caring parents. Even in her eighties, she rises before 5:00 A.M., prays, and often works until midnight or 1:00 A.M., traveling, speaking, overseeing the many mission houses she has helped to establish, and personally tending to the sick and dying. She is a dynamo of caring, and it is said that when she kneels in prayer, she is surrounded by an almost visible aura of divine power and presence.

I especially love her strong, gnarled hands. They are the hands of a worker. They have scrubbed floors, swept compounds, built fires, carried water, washed dishes, and tended wounds. They are the hands of a servant. I can imagine, someday in heaven, standing in a rollcall at which God asks to look at my hands. "Too soft!" God will say. "They have been too long at the typewriter, or too long gesturing in public speech. They should look more like Mother Teresa's hands!"

I think of someone else with the hands of a servant. I met an old Kentucky farmer one day when I was visiting my father in his retirement home. The farmer was passing through the halls, handing out apples to everyone. "In the winter," he told me, "I bring candy and chewing gum. I say, 'Here comes Santie Claus!' " I hope they let that farmer wear his overalls in heaven. I want to see him just the way he was.

I think also of a woman Tom S. Sampson wrote about in his book *Only by Grace.* She joined a church Tom pastored and wanted to do something to help others. She found a position as a volunteer in a home for older men. She hadn't worked in the home long before she saw that many of the men experienced the humiliating problem of bed-wetting in the night. So this dear woman began to rise from her own bed at 2:00 A.M. to make the rounds of the rooms, gently waking the men and reminding them to go to the bathroom. There will be stars in her crown!

And I remember Larry, a wonderful artist in the Blue Ridge mountains of Virginia, and his friend John. Larry first met John at a church dinner. John was in a wheelchair, attended by his parents. The victim of toxoplasmosis, he had already lost control of most of his body, and his head often tilted awkwardly to one side. "I knew when I saw John," said Larry, "that I loved him." He began visiting John's home and offered to keep John occasionally so his parents could get away for a rest.

As John grew worse the friendship deepened, and Larry began to take John for a month at a time, until eventually he was caring for him full-time. Patiently, he fed him, wiped his mouth, bathed him, tended him during times of illness. How gently he talked to him and stroked his forehead. Larry's own work often suffered because he was so busy with John, but he never seemed to mind. God had given him John to care for; it was as simple as that, and as beautiful.

It is easy, in a world like ours, fast-paced with achievement, entertainment, and consumerism, to forget the importance of serving. Most of us do forget. But we cannot read far in any of the Gospels without being reminded, by something Jesus said or did, that life is really empty unless it is lived for others. His whole sense of identity was tied up with being a servant.

"Unless a grain of wheat falls into the earth and dies," he said, "it remains alone; but if it dies, it bears much fruit" (John 12:24 RSV).

These words form an apt connection between the two parts of Jesus' answer to the mother of James and John. They show the relationship that often exists between serving and suffering.

THE PRICE OF SERVING

Sometimes serving carries a person not only beyond the boundaries of self-interest but also beyond the boundaries of self-preservation. There is no more dramatic picture of this in modern times than in the life of Martin Luther King, Jr. Educated in the North, he and his wife, Coretta, felt a personal preference for serving a northern church, where they could live with more human dignity. But in sympathy for southern blacks, they returned to work in Montgomery, Alabama. When leadership in the struggle for equality was thrust upon him, King at first was reluctant to accept it. It meant great public pressure, plus being away from his family much of the time. But he bowed to the necessity of his participation for the sake of others, remembering that he once had written on his seminary application that he had "an inescapable urge to serve society."

Following the success of the freedom movement in Birmingham and the publication of his book *Strength to Love,* King was tempted by an invitation from Sol Hurok Productions to abandon his work to become a highly paid lecturer around the world. His commitment to others would not let him follow this easy route, and when in November of the same year, President Kennedy was assassinated, King told his wife, "This is going to happen to me, also. You know, I don't think I will live to be forty, because this country is too sick to allow me to live."

The words were prophetic. Less than five years later, King went to Memphis to lead protesters on a march in behalf of striking sanitation workers. There was an ugly mood in the city, even among many of the blacks King was there to help. Some young blacks called out taunts, there was scuffling in the ranks, and a young man tumbled into King, knocking him to his knees in the middle of the street.

At a rally at Centenary Methodist Church, King spoke of the difficult path ahead. He didn't know what would happen to him, he said, but it didn't matter. He had been to the mountaintop; God had let him look over into the Promised Land.

"I may not get there with you," he said. "But I want you to know tonight that we as a people will get to the Promised Land. And I'm happy tonight. I'm not worried about anything. I'm not fearing any man. Mine eyes have seen the glory of the coming of the Lord!"

The next day King was dead, shot as he stood on the balcony of the Lorraine Motel. He had known it was coming. In his case, as in Jesus', it was the price of serving.

No Higher Calling

Do you suppose that the mother of James and John, when she understood what was really at stake, was reluctant to let her sons go with Jesus? Perhaps so. But we would like to believe she wasn't, that she finally comprehended the real meaning of service and realized that earthly honors are as dust, compared with the glory belonging to the servants of God.

Maybe she said, "Go, my sons, with your mother's blessing. There is no higher calling than to be a servant of Almighty God."

Sacrifice

A certain Captain Oates, with Robert F. Scott's expedition to the Antarctic, suffered severe frostbite on both feet, his condition forcing the entire party to go at a desperately slow rate. One night he said, "I am just going outside, and may be some time." He stepped out of the tent into the raging blizzard and deliberately froze to death.

It is hard for most of us to understand such a spirit of sacrifice, just as it is difficult to comprehend Jesus' teachings on self-denial. We are creatures of self-expression and self-gratification. Our only thoughts of sacrifice run to such trivial matters as going without a meal to purchase an expensive theater ticket or denying ourselves the luxury automobile we have always wanted until the last child has finally finished college. Anything more self-abasing we usually consider lunatic or ridiculous.

THE DISCIPLES' EXAMPLE

Interestingly, the same appears to have been true of the disciples of Jesus who became the pillars of the early church. Jesus tried to warn them of the approaching dangers when he saw the shadows of crucifixion closing around him, but they would have none of it. "God forbid it, Lord!" cried Peter. "This must never happen to you" (Matt. 16:22).

He might also have added, "Or to us," for when the events of that infamous night began to unfold, Peter vehemently denied that he knew Jesus or had been one of his followers.

Jesus had often taught them about the necessity of suffering and sacrifice: "You will be hated by all because of my name" (Mark 13:13). He spoke of their being arrested, flogged in the synagogues, and dragged before governors and kings (Matt. 10:17-18). "The good shepherd lays down his life for the sheep," he said (John 10:11). And the very heart of discipleship lay in these words: "If any want to become my followers, let them deny themselves and take up their cross and follow me. For those who want to save their life will lose it, and those who lose their life for my sake will find it" (Matt. 16:24-25).

Still, when the crunch came, the twelve who followed him, who knew him most intimately, were as reluctant to surrender their self-interest as we are today. They simply appeared not to understand.

Later, however, they turned completely around. According to stories that survived through the early church, many of them both lived and died sacrificially.

Sacrifice

What was the secret? What changed them from average, self-interested people into men of destiny who would face the whip or the sword for the opportunity of dying for Christ?

There was only one thing it could be: Somehow, through the death and resurrection of the Master, they had caught the vision that he had seen all along—the transcendent kingdom, the world God was bringing into reality. Peter was firm about it when he addressed the Jews at Pentecost, saying, in effect: "This Jesus, the very one you crucified, God has raised up and shown to all of us; and his Spirit has now been poured into us." Knowing what they now knew, they would live differently.

There is the secret, you see: Beholding Jesus' vision, understanding his death and resurrection, they too became servants of the vision.

FOLLOWING THE VISION

It is never easy for people without the vision to understand those who choose to follow the vision. I knew a young woman who decided to enter a convent. Because she was beautiful, everyone asked, "Why would she do such a thing? She is too beautiful to cut her hair and live behind walls!" The general opinion seemed to be that becoming a nun should be left to those who are unattractive or brokenhearted. A lovely young woman with a radiant personality was not supposed to abase herself. Yet I am sure that young woman found great happiness, for she wanted only to serve God. She wished to serve the vision.

In Hebrew, the language of the Old Testament, the

word for "servant" is *obad,* from which we derive our English word *obedience.* Jesus taught the importance of being a servant, of serving one's vision of God and the kingdom. Later, when the apostle Paul was describing for King Agrippa the manner in which he had been won over to Christ's side and become a formidable preacher of the gospel, he said, "I was not disobedient to the heavenly vision" (Acts 26:19).

This is what really leads to self-sacrifice, isn't it—the vision. Sacrifice does not begin as a desire to make an oblation of oneself. There would be something sick or abnormal in that. Karl Menninger noted in one of his books the case of a psychotic who burned his hands and feet on a scalding radiator because he wanted to bear the marks of crucifixion.

Jesus and the disciples were not like that. They did not have the "victim" mentality we have heard about, in which one goes out into the world expecting everything to be calamitous. On the contrary, they were lovers of life and joy. But when they became servants of the heavenly vision, they were inevitably propelled into events and circumstances that produced suffering. The vision brings us into conflict with the powers of this world, the structures and prejudices of society.

We can understand this, can't we? It is what happened to people in the civil-rights movement. Many were unintentionally swept up into the movement by their commitment to Christ's vision of society, Christ's care for his "little ones." Martin E. Marty, the famous church historian and writer, said, "I never expected to march anywhere for any reason, but when I heard what was happening to God's people in the deep South, I couldn't not

Sacrifice

go." He described the sense of fear he felt, walking arm-in-arm with other men and women as they approached the sullen deputies and police dogs that stood in their path. It was not anything he had ever expected to do, but his role as a servant of God carried him inexorably forward.

One night at a church camp in Arizona, I sat at dinner beside a young woman who was involved in the sanctuary movement, harboring political refugees from Central America. She was only twenty-three years old, a fresh, soft-spoken young woman who now had a police record and had been forbidden by court order to leave the state. She had no martyr's complex. She was an ordinary young follower of Jesus. But her devotion to the kingdom of God had led her to put love and her sense of duty above her own safety and welfare.

Perhaps you have read about S. Brian Willson, who was in his forties when he was suddenly catapulted into notoriety as a peace activist. A Vietnam veteran who went to college to study for the ministry and later learned Russian, hoping to join the F.B.I., Willson was haunted by the faces of women and children he had buried in Vietnam. When he went to Nicaragua and walked through areas being fought over by the contras and Sandinistas, it reminded him of Vietnam.

"My God," he said, "we're doing this again." He thought, "I must get back to the States and do everything I can to stop this."

Upon his return, he joined a group of demonstrators at the Concord Naval Weapons Station, from which munitions were loaded on ships for distribution to Central America. He was standing in front of a train bearing armaments when the engineer disregarded instructions and proceeded on the track. He has no memory of what happened, but when he awoke he was in the hospital and both his legs had been amputated below the knees. Now a symbol of the peace movement, Willson does not regret giving his limbs. "I feel that standing on those tracks," he says, "was like what we have often said the Germans didn't do [when trainloads of Jews were being sent to concentration camps]" (Los Angeles *Times*, Sept. 20, 1987).

He didn't set out to make a sacrifice; he was only being obedient to a vision.

This is always the way it is. The vision leads to obedience, and obedience leads to sacrifice. And perhaps it is fair to say that if we never make any sacrifices, it is probably because we have never really seen the vision, we have never been truly caught up in the quest for the kingdom of God.

There are many in the church who aren't caught up in the quest, but true discipleship will not be halted by that, any more than the Jesus movement was crushed by Judaism in its day. "Jesus also suffered outside the city gate"—that is, outside the area of official religion—says the book of Hebrews. "Let us then go to him outside the camp and bear the abuse he endured" (13:12-13). For the closer we are to Jesus, the more his teaching becomes real for us.

STANDING IN FOR JESUS

If one needs any confirmation of this truth, there is convincing evidence in Nikos Kazantzakis' famous novel

Sacrifice

The Greek Passion. The story is about a year in the life of the citizens of a small Greek village who are chosen to play the main parts in the annual Passion Play. Among the characters, the part of Christ is played by a simple shepherd lad, Manolios, and Judas is played by a saddler, Panayotaros.

In the course of the year, the people are so affected by the parts they are to play that they begin actually to assume those roles. When a band of wandering Greeks driven from their homes by Turks arrives in town, producing conflict with the local landowners, Manolios takes their side and earns the enmity of the townspeople. In the climactic scene, Manolios is murdered in the church on Christmas Eve by Panayotaros, acting as Judas and encouraged by the village priest.

Kazantzakis appears to be saying that anyone who seriously takes the part of Christ, and begins to think like Christ, will inevitably stand at odds with his own society at some point, and will end by being crucified in some way. This is the real origin of sacrifice. It begins not as a desire for martyrdom, but as imitation of the Master, and achieves its natural climax at the point where the ways of the Master conflict with the ways of society.

As T. S. Eliot says in *Murder in the Cathedral*, "A martyrdom is never the design of man; for the true martyr is he who has become the instrument of God, who has lost his will in the will of God, not lost it but found it, for he has found freedom in submission to God. The martyr no longer desires anything for himself, not even the glory of martyrdom."

What has Jesus taught us about sacrifice, then? Not that it is something his followers should seek, but that it is something we inevitably find by walking in the way he has shown us. And if we walk close enough to him, if our wills are lost in his, we shall not shirk the act of sacrificing. It will belong to us as naturally as it belonged to the Master.

Eternal Life

If there is a single teaching of Jesus that strikes near the very heart of human desire, it is this: eternal life. Either subliminally, masked from ourselves so that doctors of the mind must dig it out, or consciously, so that it affects our behavior almost every day, we yearn to live on and not die. James Cagney, the film star, put it this way in a couplet:

> Each man starts with his very first breath
> To devise shrewd means for outwitting death.

But we know that, in the end, death will win. So we listen with understandable longing and wistfulness to the words of Jesus: "I am the resurrection and the life. Those who believe in me, even though they die, will live, and everyone who lives and believes in me will never die" (John 11:25-26).

Yet the words are hard to comprehend in a secular, urban world like ours. They are so foreign, so mystical to people who watch television, drive on freeways, and eat frozen foods cooked in microwave ovens. We *see* death, on the TV and on the freeways. But we cannot see life beyond death, cannot get inside it and feel what it is like, cannot take its measure from where we are.

We are like the blind man I once saw sitting on a cliff above the beach, strumming his guitar as the sun was setting. The soft colors of the sunset were playing on his face. But he could not see the bright magenta globe as it settled beyond the horizon or the reds and purples of the evening clouds. Something about his face convinced me he had been blind from birth, and I suppose he had never seen a sunset. Even if I had tried to describe it, he could not have visualized it, could not have understood. It was beyond the power of his imagination, as heaven and life after death are beyond ours.

OUR NEED FOR ETERNITY

We know that we want to see and understand. It doesn't seem right to us that the gift of living should be given and then taken away. As one woman said to me, "It isn't fair. You spend your whole life learning how to live, and then when you have barely mastered the game, you have to turn in your chips!" Something in us urges us onward, toward a life that does not die.

Loren Eiseley, the anthropologist, wrote in *The Immense Journey* of once finding a catfish frozen in a wintry creek. It seemed to be staring up out of the ice, its barbels spread pathetically beside its face. On a whim, he cut the fish out, ice-block and all, and dropped it into

Eternal Life

a large can. When he arrived home, he left the can in the basement, thinking he would either dissect the fish the following day or dispose of it altogether.

Several hours later, he returned to the basement and was amazed to hear stirrings in the container where he had left the fish. He looked in. The ice had melted, and a vast, pouting mouth ringed with sensitive feelers confronted him, the gills laboring slowly but steadily.

A fishy eye gazed up at him protestingly. "A tank!" it seemed to say.

"I'll get the tank," said Eiseley, with respect.

The fish lived with Eiseley all that winter. Then, with the coming of spring, the shadow of some ancient, migratory impulse crossed a corner of its brain, and one night when no one was about, it simply jumped out of its tank. Eiseley found it dead on the floor the next morning. A million ancestral years had gone into that jump, he thought, a million years of forsaking smaller pools for larger, of leaving the muddy havens of lesser tributaries to find life in great rivers, "twining in and out through the pillared legs of drinking mammoth."

He missed the fish, which had for him a "kind of lost archaic glory," and he said, "Suppose we meet again up there in the cotton-woods in a million years or so."

I too feel a kinship to that fish, and to whatever instinct led it to leap out of its small container in search of a greater body of water. There is something in me that chafes at this mortal body as though it were a tank too small, a container too finite. I long for the life of which I have had mere intimations. Like a pioneer casting a hopeful glance at the distant mountains, I yearn for something grander beyond the horizon, some "city

115

not made with hands," as the Epistle to the Hebrews calls it.

Jesus always seems to have seen that city, to have lived with the feel of its golden streets and crystal palaces. "In my Father's house," he told the disciples, "there are many dwelling places. If it were not so, would I have told you that I go to prepare a place for you?" (John 14:2). He knew the breadth and depth of the house as if he had lived in it, had gazed from its windows and sat on its verandas. He recalled the delight of its tables, the comfort of its environs.

INSIGHTS INTO REALITY

Jesus' followers were like us. Death, to them, was real and ugly and threatening. It seemed final, like the shutting of an impenetrable shield that could not be moved, once it had fallen into place.

When Jesus went to his friends Mary and Martha, whose brother Lazarus had died, the air was filled with the cries of mourners, as was the custom, lamenting loudly the loss of a loved one to that land of caverns and deep shadows.

Jesus was patient and confident. "I am the resurrection and the life; he who believes in me, though he die, yet shall he live" (John 11:25). And, pausing for a moment before the mouth of the tomb as though not wishing to interrupt the friend beyond, he shouted, "Lazarus, come out." Then, in a momentary parting of the curtains, the stage of eternity was opened, and the dead man stepped out, as if he had been only having a cup of coffee beyond.

Eternal Life

There is where it hangs for us, doesn't it? We can imagine it, but we can't believe it. We *want* to believe it. Everything in our hearts would *like* to believe it. It would make everything so much easier if only we *could* believe it. But we never have seen it happen, or heard of it happening to anyone we know, and it strains our credulity beyond the snapping point.

That is, we *think* it does. And then we remember moments when we were not so sure, when the things we thought we knew about life and the world seemed to dissolve around us, and we caught a glimpse—only a glimpse—of the way things *might* be in the reality that lies just beyond our grasp. We recall what Einstein said—that we don't know enough yet to say precisely how things are, and one day we may know enough to sweep our hands through these earthly bodies of ours and not encounter any resistance. We recollect those wraiths of dreams or insights when we beheld loved ones who had died, or experienced our own free wanderings from the body, or sensed the presence of a higher being unfettered by the chains of time and place.

Who is to say that *these* are not the true reality, and all the "hard facts" wrong?

Once in a bookstore, I was attracted by a book. I did not buy it, and I do not remember the name of the author. But the title has haunted me on more than one occasion: *The Relevance of Bliss.* The dust jacket said it was about our moments of mystical insight—mere moments that pass in the flicking of an eyelid—which reveal to us the inner nature of life itself.

Those moments do exist, don't they? And so does that "inner nature of life itself." We often miss it because we are too busy to welcome it or too locked inside the prisons of our way of perceiving reality to suppose that there are other ways of seeing. But Jesus did not miss it, and he counseled us not to miss it either.

He spoke to Nicodemus, the thoughtful leader who came to see him, about being "born from above," so that one sees and understands what one cannot see and understand from ordinary perspectives. It was hard for Nicodemus to understand "heavenly things," Jesus said, for unlike the Son of man, he had not walked in heavenly places. But one day Nicodemus would understand, for the Son of man would be lifted on the cross as Moses had lifted a symbol of salvation in the wilderness, and whoever believed in him would have eternal life (John 3:1-15).

Eternal life. Life beyond death. Life in the midst of life. Life with a different perspective. Life that understands "the relevance of bliss." It makes a vast difference in the human situation, doesn't it?

Helen Hayes, who has left us such a beautiful legacy of theatrical memories, never forgot the pain she felt when her nineteen-year-old daughter died of polio. She wondered how she would bear the loss. At first, she was helped by the fact that so many others had experienced similar losses and had lived through them. Then, as she got in touch with her true faith, she realized it was something else that had enabled her to survive. "I believed, still do, and always will," she said, "in a life after death. I always believed in that. I always feel, when I'm tired or feeling my years, 'Ah, I'll be seeing Charlie and Mary.'"

Adela Rogers St. Johns, the best-selling author, had a similar experience when she lost her son Billy in World

Eternal Life

War II. At first she thought she would perish with grief. Then she had a brief sensation of Billy's presence and felt that he was telling her he was with God. It utterly transformed her life, and she went on to write her inspirational novel *Tell No Man*. Before she died, she wrote these words in *No Good-byes:* "I am pushing ninety. I'd be happy to stay around for another ninety years; but if I have done everything I was supposed to do in this life, I am ready to go now. It is possible that I may not be here when you are reading this. Never mind. I'll be around. Let me know if there is anything I can do for you."

KNOWING THE TRUTH

Do you think what Jesus spoke of as "eternal life" is not only life after death, life which begins when this life is done, but a new spirit of life that begins now, a spirit that changes the very manner of our living, once we have believed and been grasped by the truth? The evidence seems to support such a view.

I remember the day my mother died. I had a strange feeling of peace, as if she were nearer to me than she had ever been and knew my every thought. In the night, I dreamed of seeing her. She seemed much younger than she had been at death; she looked, in fact, as she must have looked in her thirties. She was dressed for a sea voyage, and our meeting occurred in a port where there were palm trees, though she had never seen the ocean. The ship was docked nearby and rose imposingly above the crowd mingling on the shore. When a woman who appeared to be my mother's traveling companion, a sort of guide, beckoned to her that it was time to board, we kissed and said good-bye, and they walked up the gangplank. Mother was happy and smiling, and I awoke with a beatific feeling that I have had ever since.

People wondered that I did not appear to grieve at her funeral. It was because I knew that she was alive, not dead. Knowing that made all the difference! *Knowing*— in *Walking on Water*, my friend Madeleine L'Engle says:

> We've lost much of the richness of that word. Nowadays, to know means to know with the intellect. But it is a much deeper word than that. Adam *knew* Eve. To know deeply is far more than to know consciously. In the realm of faith I *know* far more than I can believe with my finite mind. I *know* that a loving God will not abandon what he creates. I *know* that the human calling is co-creation with this power of love. I *know* that neither death, nor life, nor angels, nor principalities, nor powers, nor things present, nor things to come, nor height, nor depth, nor any other creature, shall be able to separate us from the love of God, which is in Jesus Christ our Lord.

That's the trick of it, as far as I am concerned. We *know* far more than we know we know. Jesus tried to put us in touch with what we know. And if we stay in touch with it, it will change our lives forever.

The
Second Coming

On a roadside boulder in eastern Kentucky, amateurishly scrawled in great black letters, are the words "Jesus Is Coming—Be Ready!"

High on the peak of an almost inaccessible mountain in the Andes, an Ecuadorean Indian has constructed his little house. He lives there, he says, to watch for the Lord's return.

In Rome, in a church near the Piazza di Porta Maggiore, a woman kneels fourteen hours a day. She wants to be at her prayers when the world comes to an end and Christ appears.

In a rural area of western Canada, a small group of Jehovah's Witnesses gathers each day before dawn, convinced that when Jesus returns, it will be at daybreak.

All over the world, many people believe that the Bible teaches such a return and that it will mean the end of the world as we know it. Their lives are constructed around the many sayings of Jesus about his *parousia* and the destruction of this present age.

At the same time, millions of Christians are so confused by such teachings that they have all but ceased to think about them, and they relegate the question of Christ's return to the realm of unfathomable mystery.

DISAGREEMENT AMONG THE GOSPELS

It is small wonder that there should be confusion, for the Gospels themselves do not always appear to agree on the subject.

In the Gospels of Matthew, Mark, and Luke, Jesus speaks frequently about the end of the world and his triumphant return as the ruler of a new age. His language seems unequivocal: "Truly, I say to you, there are some standing here who will not taste death before they see the Son of man coming in his kingdom" (Matt. 16:28 RSV). At times, Jesus invokes the ancient eschatological images of doom and despair:

> Immediately after the tribulation of those days the sun will be darkened, and the moon will not give its light, and the stars will fall from heaven, and the powers of the heavens will be shaken; then will appear the sign of the Son of man in heaven, and then all the tribes of the earth will mourn, and they will see the Son of man coming on the clouds of heaven with power and great glory; and he will send out his angels with a loud trumpet call, and they will gather his elect from the four winds, from one end of heaven to the other.
>
> (Matthew 24:29-31 RSV)

However, in the Gospel of John, written later than the others, the note of imminent return has been muted, and in its place is what New Testament scholar C. H. Dodd calls "realized eschatology"—the suggestion that the end of all things is not an event that will occur at a specific point in history, but a spiritual happening which already has occurred in the ministry, death, and resurrection of Christ. John's only hint of an actual return lies in Jesus' words to the disciples at the last supper: "In my Father's house there are many dwelling places. If it were not so, would I have told you that I go to prepare a place for you? And if I go and prepare a place for you, I will come again and will take you to myself, so that where I am, there you may be also" (John 14:2-3).

In this Gospel, moreover, Jesus emphasizes the sending of his Spirit to be with the disciples, and also their abiding in him and he in them. Here there is a kind of mystical blurring of the usual distinction between this life and the beyond, with the sense that Christ is never really absent from his followers, so therefore never needs to return in visible bodily form.

Admittedly, it all becomes very confusing, especially when scholars begin to compare texts and try to establish the words and intentions of Jesus that lay behind the Gospel writings. For example, in Mark 9:1, which seems to spring from the same source of Jesus' sayings as Matthew 16:28, we see: "Truly I tell you, there are some standing here who will not taste death until they see that the kingdom of God has come with power." This appears to be much more congruent with what actually happened than is the Matthean promise of the Son of man's return, if one interprets the church's experience at Pentecost as the arrival of the kingdom with power.

But which did Jesus intend? Did he expect to return

Who we will be beyond the grave
will be no different from the person
we have become on this side of the grave

M. H. Rowley

therefore: Emphasis - "Becoming...in the New!!"

in power while some of the disciples were still alive, or
was he merely predicting the success of the kingdom?

We wish we knew for sure, but obviously we don't,
and it is unlikely that the question will ever be resolved
to everyone's satisfaction—not in this lifetime, at least.

It may be better, therefore, to concentrate on what we
can learn from Jesus' teachings about the end of the
world and leave the precise manner of its occurrence to
God.

The fact that there is confusion on the subject in no
way invalidates its importance. Jesus himself warned that
the details of the matter will not be known. When the
Pharisees asked when the kingdom would come, he
answered, "The kingdom of God is not coming with signs
to be observed; nor will they say, 'Lo, here it is!' or
'There!' for behold, the kingdom of God is in the midst
of you" (Luke 17:20-21 RSV). He instructed the disciples: "They will say to you, 'Lo, there!' or 'Lo, here!' Do
not go, do not follow them. For as the lightning flashes
and lights up the sky from one side to the other, so will
the Son of man be in his day" (Luke 17:23-24 RSV).

What we must realize is that the substance of Jesus'
concern for the end of the world and his return in glory
is not altered by the apparent disagreement of the
Gospels or the failure of scholars to reach a consensus on
when these things should be accomplished.

I recall a night my family and I spent in the old walled
city of Avila, in northern Spain. On the hour, I heard several old bells ring out the time. They were never together.
One would ring, and I would begin drifting back to sleep;
then another would ring; and after that, another.

I lay there thinking about the reality of time. Time

was actually passing. I was growing older, hour by hour. But I could imagine someone arguing, "Time is not real at all, for the clocks themselves cannot agree." Such thinking would be foolish. The nonsynchronization of the clocks and bells in no way disproves the existence of time. And by the same token, confusion about what Jesus meant regarding the end of the world and his triumphant return hardly disproves the significance of the subject.

Through the entire maze of what Jesus said or is reported to have said, there are two unmistakable emphases: the importance of being ready; and, all considerations of timing aside, his eventual triumph and glory as Lord of lords and King of kings.

THE IMPORTANCE OF BEING READY

In a number of parables and sayings, Jesus stressed to the disciples the value of an alert life-style. "But about that day or hour no one knows," he said, "neither the angels in heaven, nor the Son, but only the Father."

"Beware, keep alert; for you do not know when the time will come. It is like a man going on a journey, when he leaves home and puts his slaves in charge, each with his work, and commands the doorkeeper to be on the watch. Therefore, keep awake—for you do not know when the master of the house will come, in the evening, or at midnight, or at cockcrow, or at dawn, or else he may find you asleep when he comes suddenly. And what I say to you I say to all: Keep awake." (Mark 13:33-37)

The idea of watching, waiting by the door or on a

tower, runs through all of Jesus' teachings. It has to do with inner discipline, with mentally and emotionally standing on tiptoe to be in touch with God, lest God's sudden movements take us unaware. It is good advice, whether the end of the world comes in our lifetime or not, for none of us knows when death will claim us. The important thing is that there be no disjunction between us and the eternal Spirit.

With Jesus, it was not a negative matter. We can see this in his parable of the bridesmaids. Apparently it was the custom for maidens to light the way of the bridegroom to the home of the bride. Five of the girls were disciplined and thoughtful, and had brought flasks of extra oil for their lamps; the other five brought only the oil that was in their lamps. In the celebration of the wedding, time was forgotten and the maidens all fell asleep, letting their lamps burn until the oil in them was exhausted.

Then suddenly the cry was heard: "The bridegroom is coming!" Startled awake, the girls found their lamps extinguished. The thoughtful ones merely refilled theirs from the flasks they had brought. The other girls rushed out to try to buy more oil. But while they were gone, the bridegroom arrived and the five prudent maidens escorted him to the home of the bride, where they enjoyed the great marriage feast. When the five thoughtless girls finally returned, they were denied entrance.

"Keep awake therefore," are the concluding words of the passage, "for you know neither the day nor the hour" (Matt. 25:13).

We can hardly miss the note of joy and excitement in such a story, for weddings were occasions of enormous festivity. It is true that the parable was told to warn people not to be like the foolish maidens. But the note of happiness and revelry for those who were prepared and went in to the feast is not to be missed! We are reminded to live in readiness for Christ's return—not only to avoid the consequences of being unprepared, but to enjoy the delightful consequences of being thoroughly ready, of saying, "O Lord, this is wonderful!"

When I was a young father, I often traveled a great deal, speaking across the country, and sometimes, if my assignments took me to other lands, I would be gone for several weeks. Ours was a close, happy family, and it was hard on all of us to be separated. My cards and letters, I was told, were always greeted with excitement and rejoicing, and my wife read them to the children at the kitchen table, where they gathered after school for cookies and milk.

My return, especially when I had been away for some time, was always a great occasion. My family went through the "countdown," marking off the days until I would be home. If the children were not in school, they came to the airport with my wife to meet me. When I walked down the ramp from the plane, there was squealing and shouting, and then hugs and kisses.

We always had a special meal, and there was lots of talking and catching up to do. The children reviewed everything that had occurred in school and showed me all their papers and drawings. None of us could get enough of embracing, and even after we went to bed, a glow of happiness seemed to remain in the house.

This is the sense of excitement that Jesus wanted his followers to experience when thinking about the end of the world and his return. It was not something negative to be feared and dreaded, but something beautiful and desirable, something to help us live each day in joyous expectancy. Of course, we don't know when it will be; but we can get up each morning and say, "Perhaps today will be the day! Wouldn't it be wonderful!"

THE COMING TRIUMPH

The second emphasis in Jesus' teachings on eternal life is his eventual triumph and glory as Lord of lords and King of kings. It will be wonderful because the world finally will become what God wants it to be. Creation, which will have "groaned in travail" until that moment, will suddenly burst into full flower. Paradise, understood as the experience of the first man and woman, will become the heritage of all living creatures. The crucified Lord, whom Pilate declared King of the Jews, will become King of all glory and Lord of all dominions. "Every knee should bow, in heaven and on earth and under the earth, and every tongue confess that Jesus Christ is Lord, to the glory of God the Father" (Phil. 2:10-11 RSV).

Jesus was able to live as he lived and endure what he endured because of his unshakable faith in the way things would some day be. He walked seeing the future, the time beyond time. "When the Son of man comes in his glory" was a phrase he used in teaching the disciples. He knew he must suffer pain and humiliation, even to the extent of the cross; but he also knew that God was working through him to bring about the kingdom, the renewal of all life, and he trusted God to crown him with love and glory when the redemption was accomplished. His faith never wavered.

This is why he said to the disciples, "Pay attention, keep awake," for he wanted them also to see what was ahead, and to understand, as Paul was to put it, "that the sufferings of this present time are not worth comparing with the glory about to be revealed to us" (Rom. 8:18).

We cannot even begin to picture the glory. The book of Revelation tries. After describing the cataclysm that shall occur at the end, with the powers of evil being bound and destroyed in a lake of fire, it turns to the scene in heaven, where all the saints and angels are praising God:

> Then I heard what seemed to be the voice of a great multitude, like the sound of many waters and like the sound of mighty thunderpeals, crying out,
> "Hallelujah!
> For the Lord our God the Almighty reigns.
> Let us rejoice and exult and give him the glory,
> for the marriage of the Lamb has come,
>   and his bride has made herself ready."
> (Rev. 19:6-7)

The language is similar to that favored by Jesus himself: The faithful will be gathered for a great wedding feast. Jesus is the groom and the Church is the bride. Those who belong to the Church can rejoice because they have remained faithful, they are the righteous ones of God. The careless may be locked outside, but revelry is the order of the day for those on the inside. God will unite the believers with their Lord.

"Hallelujah!"—the ancient liturgical form for "Praise

God!"—is the cry on every tongue. And why? Because "the Lord our God the Almighty reigns!"

People brought up on the King James Version of the Bible remember the ringing translation of verse 6: "The Lord God omnipotent reigneth!"

A good friend, Dr. Perry Biddle, went to preach one Sunday in a small church in Scotland. As his sermon text, he took those words—"The Lord God omnipotent reigneth"—and repeated them many times, fairly shouting them at the end.

Following the service, an officer of the church stood with him at the door to introduce him to the worshipers. When two elderly women approached, the officer explained that they were almost completely deaf. As Perry extended his hand in greeting, one woman spoke up: "I didna hear anythin' you said today, Minister, except 'The Lord God omnipotent reigneth!' But," she quickly added, "that's all that really matters, isn't it?"

It *is* all that matters! And because it is, we can live buoyantly, expectantly, leaning into the future. As the old saying has it, we may not know what the future holds, but we know Who holds the future. And knowing Jesus and his teachings, we can wait without weariness, anticipating the world's great homecoming!

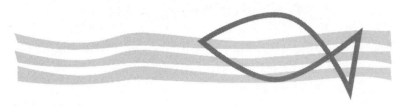

Epilogue

The teachings of Jesus, which range far beyond the main ones examined in this book, are of extraordinary scope and depth. They deal with life and death, love and hate, work and play, sin and grace—all the great paradoxes of human existence. And although Jesus never gives the appearance of being a systematic philosopher or theologian, there is absolute coherence in everything he said. Every saying fits perfectly with all the others, as if it were a small piece of a giant mosaic.

FROM AN ORAL TRADITION

The unity of his teachings is all the more remarkable when we consider that those teachings were handed down orally. Jesus never, as far as we know, wrote any of them. The only reference to his writing anything is in the story of the woman taken in adultery (John 8:1-11), when he stooped down and wrote in the sand, and even then we don't know what he wrote. Nor did any of his disciples write anything until after his death and resurrection. Thus, of all the great bodies of spiritual instruction bequeathed to history, that of Jesus is probably the only one that began entirely as an oral tradition.

The oral beginnings suggest something very special about the relationship between the teachings and the Teacher. What Jesus *said* must always be understood against the background of who he *was*. His teachings and his life were inextricably interwoven, with each informing the other from beginning to end.

Other great religious leaders—Confucius, Gautama Buddha, Muhammad—wrote down teachings that resulted from their life experiences. But with Jesus, the experiences resulted as much from the teachings as the other way around. His conflict with the authorities sprang largely from what he said about God and himself and the kingdom of heaven. The conflict led him to expand on the teachings, the expanded teachings produced greater conflict, and this vicious cycle led eventually to his crucifixion.

Jesus' teachings, unlike those of other religious leaders, may not be studied independently of his life. Once when he spoke of his coming death and of the importance of his followers' eating his flesh and drinking his blood, many of the followers, finding this a hard saying, turned away. He said to the twelve disciples, "Do you also wish to go away?" Simon Peter answered: "Lord, to whom can we go? You have the words of eternal life. We have come to believe and know that you are the Holy One of God" (John 6:67-69).

These disciples, who had spent a great deal of time

with Jesus, could not merely walk away and live by what they had learned from him. Their dependence was upon the Teacher himself, who so mystically embodied what he had taught, as the Word become flesh, that they could not finally distinguish between him and the teachings. Their commitment to who he *was* was as strong as their commitment to what he *said*.

It is a high point in the synoptic Gospels, therefore, when Jesus asks Simon Peter, "Who do you say that I am?" and Peter confesses, "You are the Messiah, the Son of the living God" (Matt. 16:15-16). Peter thus validates Jesus' teachings by recognizing that they do not come from an ordinary person but from the One whom God has made the Messiah of Israel.

There is a similar climax in the fourth Gospel, when Thomas, speaking for all believers, gives up his doubting ways to fall down before Jesus and acknowledge, "My Lord and my God!" (John 20:28). The words of Jesus are thereby seen to be "words of eternal life"—words of truer meaning and more vast significance than if Jesus had been merely a vagabond rabbi with no special relationship to God.

To Follow the Teachings
Is to Follow the Teacher

"Jesus is Lord" is said to have been the earliest creedal statement in Christendom. There would be other more elaborate statements later, but this one, strong and simple, was the bedrock of recognition upon which the entire Christian enterprise was founded.

In none of the other world religions is such a confession important. Confucius was merely a distinguished writer of proverbs and observations. Moses, who figured so distinctively in the history of his people, was primarily a revolutionary and law-giver. Buddha was a man who had learned the value of renunciation. Muhammad was an earthly leader whose teachings obviously are flawed by personal desires and ambitions.

Jesus stands alone as a Teacher who must be known and adored along with his teachings. The validity of his teachings has always been tied to what we believe about him personally. We cannot study what he said about the kingdom, or love, or sacrifice, or resurrection, without either rejecting it as sheer fancy or falling down to worship the man, as Thomas did. He does not leave us as mere eclecticists, to borrow this or that precept or principle as it suits us, but presents us with an unavoidable challenge—either to follow him or to forget what he has said.

The fact is that it is impossible to follow the teachings without following Jesus. This is what the apostle Paul discovered. "I do not do the good I want," he said, "but the evil I do not want is what I do" (Rom. 7:19). Only by surrendering himself completely to the Master, he found, could he begin to approximate the kind of life inculcated by the teachings. "I died on the cross with Christ," he wrote. "And my present life is not that of the old 'I,' but the living Christ within me. The bodily life I now live, I live believing in the Son of God who loved me and sacrificed himself for me" (Gal. 2:20 Phillips).

We are faced with a critical judgment—the one that has faced students of Jesus' teachings from the beginning. If the teachings are true, including those about

Epilogue

Jesus being the Son of God, then there is no ignoring them; we must comply, we must declare Christ our own Lord and Master.

Perhaps in the end, that is the only way to comprehend the full beauty and meaning of the teachings. For it may be with the teachings as it is with marriage—that one understands them only from within. Until one is married, one may think of the wedded state in romantic terms, or as a practical arrangement between two persons of complementary gifts. It is only after one is married that one can appreciate what it means to live daily in the rich exchange of glances, caresses, and ideas, and to know that, whatever transpires, there is always another there who cares deeply about what happens to one.

As P. T. Forsyth, the eminent theologian, has written in *The Person and Place of Jesus Christ:*

> We come, then, to our communion with God not along with Christ, and in like fashion with Christ, but *through* Christ, and *in* him. We do not believe *with* him, or by his help, but *in* him. We believe in *Him*; and *in Him* it is that we have our power to believe. He is not only faith's object but also faith's world. He becomes our universe that feels, and knows, and makes us what we are.

When does a person progress from believing that the teachings are true to believing that the Teacher is the Son of God himself? It can happen at any moment, as it did to the great literary scholar, C. S. Lewis. "I was driven to Whipsnade one sunny morning," wrote Lewis in *Surprised by Joy.* "When we set out I did not believe that Jesus Christ is the Son of God, and when we reached the zoo I did."

135

Needless to say, it is a moment of the most profound significance, for afterward, nothing is ever again the same. The teachings are seen in a new dimension, and life itself takes on an incredible radiance. "Following Jesus" is no longer a rhetorical phrase, something previously relegated to zealots and fanatics; it becomes instead a way of being that leads to blessedness and fulfillment.

Albert Schweitzer put it most beautifully, I think, in the final sentences of *The Quest of the Historical Jesus:*

> He comes to us as One unknown, without a name, as of old, by the lake-side, He came to those who knew Him not. He speaks to us the same word, "Follow thou Me!" and sets us to the task which He has to fulfill for our time. He commands. And to those who obey Him, whether they be wise or simple, He will reveal Himself in the toils, the conflicts, the sufferings which they shall pass through in His fellowship, and, as an ineffable mystery, they shall learn in their own experience Who He is.